WINDOWS
RESTAURANT

Bon
Appetite!

WINDOWS RESTAURANT

Talk About Good!

P H I L I P   M U R R A Y

MariPhil, Inc.

Traverse City, Michigan

MariPhil, Inc., dba Windows Restaurant
7677 West Bay Shore Dr.
Traverse City, MI 49684
pmurray@infinitecom.com
www.windowstc.com

Publisher's Cataloging-in-Publication Data

Murray, Philip.
    Windows Restaurant : Talk About Good! by Philip Murray
        p. ill. cm.
    Includes index.
    ISBN 0-9709572-0-3
        1. Cookery, American. 2. Cookery, Michigan.
        3. Food Preparation—regional. 4. Specialty, recipes.
    I. Title.
        TX715.2L68B36 2002
        641.59763–dc21

PROJECT COORDINATION: Alexander W. Moore, Jr.
BOOK DESIGN: Barbara Hodge

06 05 04 03 ❖ 5 4 3 2 1

Printed in Canada

Dedicated to the Loving Memory of

JOHN JOSEPH MURRAY, JR.
a.k.a.
"Jack"
"Uncle Johnny"

A big brother who always told me I was going to make it,
and whenever he went out to eat,
"Windows was his standard."

Contents

In Appreciation

Marilyn Foren Murray

Floyd and Clara Foren

Marion Murray

Mari Patton Chamberlain

Randy Chamberlain

Dewayne and Cheryl Litwiller

Cory Luna

Sally Towner

Bill Power

Brad Chaplin

Jessica Mayjzak

Tracey Gillmore

Laura Banks

Rolf Schliess

Patti Haven

Joni Capling

Kevin Nummerdor

Claud Mills

Matt Sivits

Bill Cataldo

Malcolm and Chantal
Gaines and Sharron

John and Ann Marie Mitchell

Micheline Cazayoux

Chef Leonard Stec

Chef Van

Chef Benson

Chef Michael Cannon

Ned Duke

Toni Viet

Steve Marovich

Fuzzy

Paul Pruhdomme

Paul Miller

Daniel Bonnot

Jean Campagni

Frank Brightsen

Lori Steele

Frank Lerchen

Frank Noverr

Ron Williamson

Ken Blackstone

Rhys Moore

Ted Mac Manus

Jim and Becky Stacy

Jim Milliman

Dick Rosa

Photographers

Glen Graves

Tom Kachadurian

Steve Ballance

The Guernsey Dairy boys

Ziggy

Mary Boudjalis

May and Doc

Becky Phipps

Dennis & Charlene Debest

Mark Dressler

Mike Cole

Dan Clark

Rodney Himmel

Ron Ernsberger

Steve Hogan

Liz Vogel

Tim Middaugh

Don Leone

Sherri Hill Asper

Bud Cline

Alex Moore

Richard and Susan Kuschell

The staff at
Traverse the Magazine

Especially the wonderful
and very appreciated
Windows' clientele

WINDOWS
RESTAURANT

Introduction

My future appeared as I was washing dishes at Mondo's Restaurant. I was a fifteen-year-old high school sophomore, new to restaurants and struggling to keep pace with the incoming stacks of Saturday morning breakfast platters. I picked up a dirty plate. There, stuck by dried egg on the bottom, was a five-dollar bill. I had a revelation: I wanted to be a chef.

People everywhere liked to eat—and I would feed them. I could go anywhere in the world. During our fifteen-minute break, I slathered up crispy hash browns with butter and ketchup and daydreamed about being a chef, about travel and adventure. I talked about saving up money for a car. I would travel the globe cooking.

I didn't know then that the journey to become a chef would take me through more than fifteen restaurant kitchens from the Gulf of Mexico to New England to the upper Midwest. I didn't know I would burn toast in diners, sauté alongside celebrity chefs, learn classic techniques from European chefs, and finally, with my wife, open our own restaurant on West Grand Traverse Bay in Leelanau County, Michigan. All I knew, when I saw that five-dollar bill stuck to a plate in Mondo's stainless steel sink, was that I wanted to be able to move through a kitchen like my classmate Ron Lipa.

Ron was the cook at Mondo's, a family restaurant with vinyl booths and white formica tables in Roseville, Michigan, a Detroit suburb filled with greasers and tough guys. Ron had it all together: flawless deluxe burgers, tricky eggs over easy and precision-stacked club sandwiches. He made orchestrating plate lunches and hearty breakfasts appear so easy, so effortless. As I watched him on my first day at work, I envied his abilities.

Meanwhile, I fought at the sink as the wait staff dumped dishes through a small stainless steel hole in the wall. My white apron was wet from sudsy water, and the dishes kept coming. There were coffee cups, forks, plates, saucers, platters, spoons. I battled to keep up, and finally, hours later, the piles diminished. I was just about done. But no. Ron began piling up the remains of the day: pots, sauté pans, spatulas, fryer baskets and greasy utensils. I turned from the pile and watched as he scrubbed the grill with pumice and splashed water over it. Steam billowed from the surface. Ron gave a last shiny wipe and turned away.

"See ya!" he said, and fled Mondo's.

I spent the next half-hour scrubbing, dreaming about quitting time. I figured I'd be home soon. But no. The owner appeared with a mop and bucket, and I looked down, scanning the floor. There was more food on it than a Greyhound bus buffet. I began picking up the stinky mats, rinsing them and mopping the floor. I finished at about 10:30 p.m. and raced home, collapsing in bed.

Morning came early. I woke up achy and exhausted at 6:30 a.m. for driver's training, wondering, How could they make me do all of that work my first night? But, at $1.25 an hour, I felt I could stick it out.

The next night was harder. As I closed the restaurant again, cleaning mats and mopping the floor, I wondered, How could Ron be such a good cook and work the primo hours, while I get stuck with the dredges of the restaurant? The next morning I sat in back of a driver's training car heading through Clinton Township, outside Detroit, toward Anchor Bay. "Backseat drivers end up in the trunk," the instructor instructed. I tried to pay attention, but I dozed off. When the car stopped, I perked up. I was drooling, and it was my turn to steer.

Over the next few months the enthusiasm for my career choice burned in me. I was determined. Still, I had to make it through two years of high school—a seemingly endless stretch of time. I learned about Schoolcraft College and I mailed an application. There was a three-year wait to enter its acclaimed culinary arts program. Things were working out perfectly: I could graduate and head straight into cooking.

When my father moved the family from St. Clair Shores to Plymouth the following year, I was living a mere fifteen minutes from Schoolcraft. My life was set. Once I learned how to cook I could live anywhere; I could travel and explore the world.

After graduating in June 1973, I was eager to start my culinary career the following fall, with my father's blessings and support. While my anticipation for going to chef school was coming to fruition, I lived at home with my parents.

"Son, if you wish to go to college you can live at the house for free," he told me, "but you have to pay your own way."

"Gee, thanks, dad."

I thanked my father for being a lifesaver.

I scouted restaurants in Plymouth for a new job, but most wouldn't hire anyone under age eighteen. My parents, meanwhile, had grown a little concerned at my fascination with becoming a chef, and, when I took a janitor's job at a nearby nursing home, I figured it would be a test of my resolve. I scrubbed floors on my hands and knees and waxed them until I became an orderly. Mr. White would sing, "Jesus loves me, yes I know" while the Popa Booshska lady kept rhythm. A slight shaving nick on Alex summoned the ambulance. I enjoyed the adventure of working at the nursing home, but soon it was time to start cooking school. I was chomping at the bit.

Later, however, my father suddenly and unexpectedly passed away. As is often the case, my father's death pitched the family into financial and emotional crisis. My father had recently purchased his own service company that cleaned, installed and maintained draft beer systems in businesses and private homes. My brothers and I decided to keep the business operating, and before I knew it, my chef dreams were on hold. I wanted to pursue my own destiny but wasn't able to attend classes. I drove myself and others mad.

I realized I could take classes part time until I could figure a way out. My route, meanwhile, was taking me to some of the very types of places I would eventually work as a cook, to upscale restaurants, hotels, country clubs and oyster bars in Ann Arbor and the Detroit area. As I cleaned beer lines I would seek out the chefs, and then I'd start volleying questions.

"What are your best-selling entrees?" I'd ask.

"What kind of fish is that?"

"What's in the soup?"

This detour from culinary college became part of my schooling. The chefs told me their work was rewarding and exciting, and the positive encouragement nourished my resolve to work with food. The following year, I finally left the beer business and started classes at Schoolcraft College. That was it: I was in. I was on my way. I was happy as a clam.

My phenomenal first year began with the sixteen-week production section, headed by Chef Benson, in which we learned the art of preparing food in bulk. We studied menus, developed recipes and estimated volumes required for feeding fifty to 500 people at banquets and parties. Benson had more energy than three people, and everything was quick like a bunny. He loved the food business. This chef was the king of MUSKO—his term for turning leftovers into meals. He could open a refrigerator, pull out any remains and create a new, odd dish. He utilized everything. Although I had no experience, some of Benson's food combinations were really stretching it, such as turning leftover sausage, broccoli, soup, ham, onions, tomato sauce and cheese into a new creation. But it was, all in all, a good learning experience. After all, we fed the school cafeteria.

During some of the first-year academics, we were pounded in class about the importance of sanitation and food safety. I could tell these chefs were not going to let us do anything in the kitchen until we finished food safety and sanitation classes.

Second-year students with Benson moved beyond the cafeteria to more elegant and exciting parties. Fliers announcing monthly gourmet nights, which we prepared, went out to the community and college staff and students, and we occasionally cooked for special parties at the home of Schoolcraft College's president. At the time, I was renting a house next to the college, filling my schedule with wrestling, piano, and art classes. The time I'd spent working for the family beer business taught me that I'd be working hard the rest of my life after college. So I decided to have fun. Meanwhile, other culinary students devoted forty hours a week to restaurant work.

Benson teased us about what we'd be doing in ten years.

"Jerry is going to be a manager of Little Caesar's," he joked, "and Tim will be a five-star resort hotel chef."

When he came to me, he simply pointed his finger and shook his head.

Although I felt I was moving steadily toward my goal of being a chef, my instructors believed otherwise. If I was not working full time at some restaurant, it seemed to them I was not totally committed to the career of a chef. Nonetheless, I continued toward my goals.

Schoolcraft's pastry chef, Len Stec, headed up the next section of culinary classes, and his portion of the kitchen was a laboratory. It was spotless. Impeccable. Whenever we baked or cooked, whenever we touched anything, it had to be cleaned right away. Stec was classically trained in the grand hotel style of the 1940s and 1950s, but unfortunately many of his techniques are no longer taught in culinary schools. He had a thousand recipes. We learned Stec's purist and involved approach to making chiffon cakes by meticulously beating egg whites, and we steeped fresh fruit to make fillings for pies and tarts. We made many desserts, pastries, and learned basics that I would work from for years. Under Stec's guidance, I made a classic Black Forest Torte for my sister Becky's tenth birthday. My family had grown up with traditional Mid-American fare—fried chicken or roast beef, mashed potatoes and vegetables on Sundays—and my father's Army cooking—fried rice and scrambled eggs or chipped beef on toast—on some weeknights. They were awed by Becky's birthday cake: twelve layers of chocolate chiffon cake, crisp puff pastry, lots of whipped cream, sweet cherries and chocolate shavings.

For the school's culinary arts show, I partnered with Skip, who was a believer like me, a wanna-be chef in the making. We decided on turkey chaud-froid. This involved roasting and chilling a turkey, glazing it with aspic—a mayonnaise-gelatin mixture—then lavishly decorating it with vegetable cutouts. Skip and I proceeded for the next four hours on our first culinary creation.

After the turkey was roasted, we put it in the cooler to chill. We then made our chaud-froid: mixing gelatin in cold water first and then stirring it into boiling water as the rapids were dying down. We placed the gelatin mixture in a bain-marie, which is a water bath similar to double boiling, then placed the bain-marie into an ice bath and cooled it to room temperature. We added mayonnaise and stirred the cooling sea of mayonnaise and Jell-O, perfectly tempered to coat the golden-roasted turkey. The first coat was similar to a whitewash or primer. The second through fourth coats were a super lacquered finish that coated the turkey completely. Left alone with some fresh parsley, cranberries, chestnut dressing and Dairy Queen mashed potatoes, it would have been a real winner. Instead, Skip and I prepared carrots, sweet peppers, poached green scallion greens and olives, all perfectly cut into quarter-inch diamonds. We spent three hours individually dipping each vegetable in clear gelatin to make a turkey that would have made Liberace proud.

When showtime arrived, the display was quite warm. Before long the mayonnaise-Jell-O coating started to melt and, with the weight of all the vegetables, produced a landslide.

My final sixteen weeks were with the infamous Chef Van, who taught meat cutting, vegetable preparation and garde manger classes. He had a reputation for being strict and hard to please. The first day in class he gave me a 202 pan, which is two inches deep, twenty-four inches long and twelve inches wide. Chef Van told me to go in the walk-in refrigerator and get three bunches of celery, six onions and six peppers. I came back with the 202 pan under my arm and the onions in my apron, barely holding on to the celery and peppers.

"What do you think the 202 pan is for?" he asked.

The next day we worked on vegetable cutting to make ten gallons of Mulligatawny soup, which called for lots of finely diced vegetables. I was getting the hang of the French knife and was halfway through a huge pile of perfectly diced celery when I cut into myself. The quarter-inch slice off the tip of my thumb shocked me. I thought I was going to bleed to death.

No wait, I thought to myself, I'll wait until I regain my composure and then tell the chef I cut myself.

He couldn't possibly give me any guff about that, I thought. So I waited. My towel was turning red. My thumb was starting to throb.

"Chef," I finally said, "I cut my thumb."

He did not look at me but instead kept gazing at his beloved vegetables.

"Did you cut a piece off?" he asked.

"I think I did."

"What do you mean? Let me see that cut."

Everybody stopped what they were doing. All eyes were on me. I felt nauseated and sick, and I prepared for Chef Van to chastise me.

"You are not going anywhere," he finally said, "until you find that chunk of your thumb. I will not have any of your flesh in my soup. You will stay here and find it."

I spent twenty minutes digging through ten pounds of diced celery as my thumb bled into the towel. When I found it, and with proper identification, Chef Van allowed me to walk down to the nurse's office to get bandaged. When I returned, Chef Van threw out the tainted celery and the class diced another ten pounds for Mulligatawny soup.

When summer break hit, I was ready for work in restaurants. I had to find a place that was within biking distance. I applied to any within thirty to forty-five minutes of my home, certain my enthusiasm and my year of culinary classes would guarantee an employer. But no. I had no real experience. I went to Northville Charlie's, the Hilton—everyone said no dice. I finally found a job at the Clock Restaurant, a short-order diner where I started at $4 an hour as the "toast dude." I figured what the heck, I needed to pick up my speed and consistency. Why not work short order? I started on a Sunday and it was really busy. They were slammed. But being the toast dude seemed easy enough: the white and wheat bread went through the conveyor toaster once; the rye bread went through twice. Easy enough? I ended up with pieces of burnt wheat, burnt white and warm ryes. I was promptly dismissed at the end of my shift.

The firing was discouraging. I kept to myself. I started reading Auguste Escoffier's culinary bible, *Le Guide Culinaire*. Throughout my career I have returned to this masterpiece, each time gaining techniques and ideas for garnishes, recipes, preparation. Reading this master Frenchman buoyed my spirits and I knew I would come out ahead. Striding into Great Scots supermarket, I applied to be a meat cutter.

"Get lost," they said politely.

At the nearby Guernsey Farms Dairy restaurant—a large family farm with a dairy, truckloads of milk and homemade ice cream—I was finally hired as a breakfast and lunch cook. The 6 a.m. to 2 p.m. shift was ideal, and I could bike to work. My first days on the job I was lost, but then I remembered my old mentor, Ron Lipa, and the memory of his efficiency at Mondo's kept me focused. Feeding the six or seven Guernsey boys was my main objective. They ordered massive breakfasts—three eggs, a pound of ham, hash browns, double orders of toast—and if things went wrong in the kitchen, they always gave me another chance. I developed my own chicken and rice soup, beaming with pride at my first commercial culinary act. Lunch crowds grew over the summer. I was in heaven, cooking every day.

During my years at Schoolcraft, I lived within walking distance of college in a three-bedroom ranch with a biker who worked at Ford Motor Co. I'd come home, make a batch of chicken stock and offer them some of my dear chicken soup. My roommate, his girlfriend and biker buddies would just look at me as if I were speaking a foreign language. But back at school, I was entering the final phase of education before becoming a chef. Classes turned into intellectual battlegrounds. I sat listening to arguments on hollandaise sauce preparation: "For every three egg yolks there needs to be a half eggshell full of beef consomme." The discussion's intensity was similar to talks on detente and the Cold War.

I completed my culinary studies in 1977 and took away three very memorable lessons: Good sanitation—a clean, sterile work environment—is crucial in restaurants, unless you want to make everyone ill. Secondly, largely due to losing my fingertip, I learned the importance of carefully handling knives. And finally, I remember the first question on my final exam: "Name 25 kinds of cheeses." I answered: "American, Swiss, Velveeta, Velveeta with pimento, blue cheese, blue cheese crumbles ..."

With my lessons in hand, I needed to find a job close to home, and I became the new head chef at Papa Gepetto's. Though I'd never cooked Italian before, I perfected the job within two weeks. Entrées came out perfectly timed, the garlic bread was toasted to order, and my five workers were making fabulous meatballs. The owner was secretive about his ingredients, and as I diced vegetables I'd watch him sprinkle dried herbs and onion salt in tomato-based sauces. But things here didn't last long. The owner kept charging me for soda pop and coffee, and it was time to move on to new challenges.

I had never seen a kitchen like the one at the Wagon Wheel Steakhouse. The chef was so organized, he had outlined all the hanging utensils in Magic Marker so we knew where everything went. I trained for two days and went to work with a helper on a Friday night, making strip steaks and filets, thick-cut fries and baked potatoes. My helper handled the French dip sandwiches and iceberg lettuce salads. As he worked on a French dip, I grabbed the French knife so I could slice the sandwich. I turned abruptly and the knife landed the middle of my helper's arm. I had never heard someone scream so loud. After sending him to the hospital in a taxi cab, I finished the shift, recooking quite a few steaks that were returned overcooked. The next morning the telephone rang.

"You're fired," my boss said.

My helper needed several stitches. It was just the beginning of humility for me. The frustration of the restaurant business—from burnt toast to knife wounds—was wearing me down. Still, I realized it was all part of the learning process.

I saw a classified ad for the Hilton Hotel and tried applying again. The chef was gregarious, interested in my résumé and he held out an extra hand. He saw that I wanted to be a chef. The 3 p.m. to 11 p.m. shift was perfect, and it was full time. When I showed up for work, I went to train with Ralph. He was about six-foot five-inches tall and delighted to have a slave.

"First things first," he said. "Let's go to the upstairs walk-in and check out our inventories, make a requisition list, make a prep list. Let's get to work."

Whatever that means, I thought.

Ralph headed into the walk-in and waited for me to enter. He closed the door. Ralph then grabbed the red cooking wine and started guzzling it down, thirstily.

"Here," he said, handing it to me. "Try some. You're going to need it to get through the night."

"No thanks," I told him, and headed back to the kitchen.

I started training on the sauté station, setting it up with chicken breasts, veal, rainbow trout, stocks, wine, and an overwhelming variety of vegetable garnishes. When orders started coming in, we had about six sauté pans going at once with orders for twenty-five or thirty more dinners waiting to be cooked. This was the most confusing part of cooking. How could they possibly cook all this food and cook it right? Jim, the sauté chef that trained me, was very experienced. At one point, he instructed me to stand aside while he sautéed. It took about a week to work the station by myself. It was very challenging, and concentration levels had to be at peak or I'd soon get in the weeds.

Within a month I had mastered the sauté station and was ready for more. I begged and pleaded with the chef to put me on the broiler—the hardest station to work. Many had tried, and many had failed. On that thirty-inch grill, everything had to be cooked perfectly: all the mediums, the wells, the medium-wells, the rares. A semi-retired executive chef in his mid-thirties trained me. He was changing careers and becoming a veterinarian. He thought cooking was for the birds, and he tried to discourage me. I tuned him out.

"The only rewarding thing is sitting in an office, eating lobster tail," he told me.

Nine months passed quickly at the Hilton, and though I'd been through every station in the kitchen, I knew I still had plenty to learn about cooking. I again picked up Escoffier and the reading inspired me to develop new specials like tournedos Rossini, a tenderloin steak with a foie gras, truffles and demi-glace sauce. I started working banquets with the chef and found, with the volume of cooking, I couldn't focus attention on each and every dinner.

One day the chef asked me if I would like to cook breakfast on the weekends at the pool-side cafe.

"What the heck," I said. "I could use some weekend nights off."

I showed up at the tiny kitchen thirty minutes before opening. There was no food at all. I had one helper. He had no experience. The wait staff opened the doors—my helper was out getting bacon, eggs, bread and whatever else he could find—and within ten minutes all 250 seats filled up. Everybody wanted breakfast. I was horrified. There was no way these people could be fed. It would be dinnertime before they got their breakfast. I closed down the kitchen and went back home to bed. The chef was fuming, but I was equally mad because he hadn't prepared me for the pool-side situation. Soon, I departed.

A posh, upper-crust Ann Arbor country club was my next adventure. This was my first experience with a real chef. I was hired in as a sauté chef and would be cooking gourmet dinners to order. This was right up my alley. I was really excited. This was a state-of-the-art kitchen with a great design. But after too many little scoops of Haagen-Dazs boysenberry sorbet with mint, after too many new ways to cook roast beef, I was on my way.

A new high-fashioned eatery, Leopold Bloom's, had recently opened in Ann Arbor, home of the University of Michigan. Decorated with Tiffany lamps, antiques and Louis Icahn prints, Leopold Bloom's contained private booths with etched glass panels. This was true gourmet, an Alice in Wonderland of restaurants. They took me on as a sauté chef, and I became part of an eclectic, university town staff.

The dishwasher was a linguist who spoke five languages and studied Chinese between washing pots and pans. Murphy, a cook, had his own kitchen philosophy: "If it's smoking, it's cooking. If it's black, it's done." One waitress with a doctorate in philosophy could never find the butter scoop. Fuzzy was the grizzly bear of cooks. He was very grouchy at first but, once I worked with him, his good heart was apparent. Steve, the over-educated intellectual, was a wild sports fanatic and a part-time cab driver when he wasn't working Leopold's salad station making the famous tiptoe through the garden salad. Steve was the poor soul that, in 1986, I talked into coming to Traverse City to help open up Window's Restaurant. Steve was a great help and very instrumental in perfecting our dauphinoise potato recipe and in helping the restaurant's overall success.

Added together, Leopold Bloom's staff probably totaled 100 years of university schooling. With my lowly two-year education, I felt a little insecure. It didn't really matter because all I had on my mind was food.

On my first day, I trained with Fuzzy and Tom Space. Tom showed me some garlic butter—raw cloves floating in a container of oil.

"What do we use this for?" I asked.

Fuzzy gruffly turned to me. "That's how we do things," he said.

Leopold Bloom's staff was very serious about food, but it was a fun place to work, the type of place where we debated the virtues of fresh vs. dehydrated parsley and where staff gave pet names to refrigerators: "Wanda" held all of the produce; "Larry" held meat and beer.

During my tenure at Leopold's, everyone loved great food. Every day was a new recipe, a new style, a new idea. I was working 80 hours a week, living and breathing the place, and reading Escoffier in my off hours, dreaming of new dishes, sauces and garnishes. With Steve and Liz and everybody else, we were rocking some really good food. It was some of the most fun that anyone could ever have in a kitchen. But I was 22 years old and I knew I needed more experience. Leopold's was going gangbusters.

I hired a new chef who was twice my age and had three times as much experience. But I figured it would really help out the restaurant. Then, in one day, my boss saw that this new chef wanted my job. I was fired by the end of the week. My girlfriend and I broke up, and I received the final nail in the coffin by losing my driving privileges for the remainder of the century.

I went home, and in the mail was my latest issue of *Bon Appetit* magazine. Chef Paul Prudhomme was on the cover.

I quickly put together my résumé and mailed it to a few restaurants in New Orleans, Louisiana, including Commander's Palace, where Chef Prudhomme worked, Galatoire's and Antoine's. Two days later I was on the highway, headed to New Orleans. It was an unforgettable drive through uncharted, unfamiliar territory. After two days on the road I saw a sign: "New Orleans, 110 Miles." The rush of excitement and anticipation is still vivid. On the outskirts of New Orleans was an exit for "Chef Highway." That was it. Here was a city that named roads after chefs. It was unbelievable.

I pulled off on Chef Highway and rented a cheap motel room. I was psyched and began mapping out my plan of attack. I'd never get directly hired at Commander's Palace, I figured, so I would first try Galatoire's, a classic French Creole restaurant with starched white tablecloths and elegant mirrors on the walls. The next morning I walked in and introduced myself. Yes, they had received my résumé. Yes, I could start right away, but only for $6 an hour. I politely declined and was off to Antoine's. They were not hiring. I walked around the French Quarter for a few hours, ate a late lunch, then drove back to my seedy motel on Chef Highway. I kept thinking, Did I make a mistake coming down here? I already missed home.

The next morning I was up in the Garden District about 9 a.m. and finally found Commander's Palace. I meekly walked in the only open door near the kitchen. This place was mammoth, a Southern mansion and former bordello that had been converted into a restaurant. Across the street was a huge cemetery filled with above-ground tombs and elaborate monuments. New Orleans was eerie. As I wandered into the kitchen, I saw only one chef, partially hidden behind the line.

I finally spoke up.

"Good morning," I said. I was trying to be positive. First impressions always count.

"Good morning," he replied. "Can I help you?"

"My name is Phil Murray and I would like to speak to Chef Paul Prudhomme."

"My name is Armand, nice to meet you. Are you looking for a kitchen job?"

"Yes."

"Can you read and write?"

"Sure I can."

"Then you won't have a problem getting hired here. Chef Paul will be in around noon."

I was hopping with excitement. I paced. I walked. For two hours, I explored New Orlean's fabled Garden District, past Victorian mansions with sculpted wrought iron fences, lush landscapes and Gothic above-ground cemeteries. The whole time I couldn't wait to meet a chef who had made the cover of *Bon Appetit*.

When we finally met, the soft-spoken, personable Prudhomme said he had received my résumé. Within five minutes he asked when I could start working.

"How much do you need to live on?" he asked.

I was so eager to work with him, I underquoted my salary requirements. It still kept me at just above the poverty line and kept me humble. I had driven south from Ann Arbor on a Tuesday and was working the sauté station at Commander's Palace on Friday. I had found a city where chefs were famous and where fine cuisine commanded respect. I had found my Garden of Eden.

Cooking at Commander's Palace was a phenomenon. There were four line cooks, two to three back-line cooks, and a sous chef named Jim Miller who made Gen. George S. Patton seem tender. Jim demanded perfection and quality. From the moment I walked in, he was on me and absolutely nothing got by him. When he learned I was from Michigan—a Yankee—I was cast into a deep abyss of disrespect.

My first task at Commander's Palace was peeling fifty pounds of carrots and slicing them in the exact same way. It was unrelenting. By about 5 p.m., the staff's food was ready and I was starved. My first real taste of Southern cooking was this staff meal: black-eyed peas with ham hocks, andouille sausage, crispy French bread with butter, and pecan pie. I sat in the garden courtyard to eat, surrounded by ferns, azaleas, and Spanish moss. I was about two bites into this fine meal when my boss walked over.

"You've got thirty seconds to finish eating," he said. "Then back to work."

I was ready. Training began with Henry, a black gentleman in his late thirties whose disposition was, in his own words, like a helpful, older woman. He was good. As I watched him cooking, I felt overwhelmed. The sauté station just hummed along. The massive kitchen was synchronized to feed gourmet meals to 600 diners each night. Vegetables were timed perfectly to be ready with the entrées. This place was flawless. A full-time butcher cut the beef and veal and also portioned the fish. It was an amazing operation.

Paul Prudhomme finally made his appearance in the kitchen. The portly chef sat on a stool and watched the food go out. From his post, he offered cooking suggestions to everyone and, from fifty feet away, would point out when a cook missed a scale on a fish.

Two weeks passed before Jim let me sauté. Another month went by before I had the station under control. Every day I learned something new. The seafood at Commander's Palace was so fresh that some was still warm from the Gulf of Mexico or Mississippi River. I soon moved to the broiler, one of the hardest positions I had ever worked. Six workers had come and gone in sixty days, unable to handle the pressure of the broiler. My hard-core boss, Jim, stood over me to ensure that nothing would be overcooked, from my tomatoes Provencal; to carved, squashed and turned mushrooms; oven-roasted redfish Greig; baked speckled trout; luscious crab imperial; crab au gratin (made with American cheese, please!); broiled Chateaubriand; tournedos; filet mignon; and huge New York strip steaks. Put together with 600 people a night, it was a lot of work.

In the early afternoons, many of the restaurant's ingredients were delivered. One gentleman brought strictly crab meat, fresh picked, for the redfish and veal. Others supplied fresh crawfish for bisque or crawfish magnifique. Fresh, huge, succulent soft-shell crabs would arrive crawling around in a box, later to be cleaned, lightly seasoned with Creole spices, dipped in flour, egg-washed and floured again. The crab were hung on a pole so their legs hung down. The legs were first fried to stiffen them. Then the whole crabs were dropped in the fryer. Once crispy and golden brown, the legs stood straight up, and a red-hued Choron sauce garnished the center of the body.

One afternoon, three men brought in a massive, 150-pound three-foot turtle in a washtub. I couldn't figure out what was going on. They dumped it into a sink, then Jim started smacking the turtle on the head. Someone else reached over and sliced the turtle's throat.

"What is this all about?" I asked, furious.

"They're making turtle soup."

I had seen everything.

After about two months, I started to make friends and felt like I was fitting in. I moved out of the Chef Highway motel to a studio apartment within walking distance to Commander's Palace. It was small—I could lay on the bed and touch the refrigerator with one foot and the front door with the other foot—and I was broke, but I was learning about cooking every day. I didn't have a TV or stereo so I often stayed home and studied Escoffier. Thanksgiving was coming and it fell on my day off. I volunteered to work.

"No," Jim said. "Stay home. We don't need you."

"I'll work for free," I offered.

He still said no. So on Thanksgiving I sat in my apartment reading *Kelley's Heroes*, a World War II novel, and eating peanut butter and bread crust sandwiches. I wanted to go home. When I went back to work, I requested a few days off during Christmas. Jim thought it was outrageous.

"There's no way you're going anywhere," he said. "Get back to work."

I cried while peeling tomatoes. The restaurant was unrelenting. The concentration level always had to be at peak. I finally broke down and talked to Chef Paul Prudhomme, asking him if I could please have a few days off at Christmas. When he agreed, Jim had a fit. He rode me harder and I could tell he was trying to make me quit. That just made me try even more.

I counted the days until Christmas and managed to take a whole paycheck to buy a plane ticket. Before leaving I picked up some andouille sausage, crab meat, and other Louisiana goodies. When my mother picked me up at the airport, I was wearing a Hawaiian shirt, sandals, and no coat. It was wintry December in Detroit. I was freezing, but I didn't care. I was home. On Christmas morning, I made sausage omelets for my family and also cooked jambalaya and gumbo to rave reviews. I felt bonded. I felt loved once again. I was ready to return to New Orleans. The day I got back, my mom called me and told me to come back and scrape the dried egg off her ceiling.

I made some lifelong friends in New Orleans, including a smart-as-a-whip Mississippi man named Gaines, a cook who was best man at my wedding. He was filled with Southern aphorisms: "Boy, you're dumber than wood."

Frank Brigtsen, who worked at Commander's Palace, eventually roomed with me near Tulane University. He stayed with Paul Prudhomme until he opened up Brigtsen's Restaurant, a successful cutting-edge Creole restaurant. Malcolm, the kitchen expeditor, was an East Coast intellectual who always had answers on the tip of his tongue. Malcolm believed in me and continually challenged me to complete my lofty goal of becoming a chef.

Some of Windows' current and past menu items hail from long nights with Gaines, Frank, Malcolm, and I drinking cheap beer and shooting pool at the China Doll Bar. Among the dishes are our Veal Winn Dixie—veal with artichokes, mushrooms, lobster and jalapeño butter—and tournedo China Doll, a center-cut tenderloin, pan seared and garnished with foie gras in truffle butter, and fresh sautéed morel mushrooms.

The Brennen family ran Commander's Palace, and it was a tight ship. Ella was the most vibrant of them all. One night I was busily working the broiler preparing tournedos coliseum, two petite filet grilled with different sauces: bearnaise and marchands de vin, the latter of which inspired tournedo Nicholas on Windows' menu. As I was grilling, Ella Brennen walked past and shouted at me.

"What do you call that?"

"It's a well-done steak," I said.

"Well that looks terrible. Make another one!"

The following week, I was busy working the broiler and sous chef Jim Miller demanded I start grilling a Chateaubriand. I started cooking it but was busy with other items.

"Don't burn that," he said. "It's very VIP."

"Yeah, yeah," I thought. I didn't see an order for it.

When that very-VIP Chateaubriand was finished, it went to Ella's sister, Adelaide Brennen. I later learned it was for her dog. I couldn't believe it. I was cooking for a rich pet.

After close to a year, I'd learned most everything I could at Commander's Palace. I would miss the best part of the job: the nightly employee dinner in the courtyard. If I was prepped, I could sit in the luscious garden and eat, energized by the smell of Southern flora. But it was time to move along.

My next adventure was very short. Two weeks to be exact. It was at the Court of Two Sisters, a pricey tourist-oriented restaurant in the French Quarter that served 300 to 400 people each night. They hired me as a sous chef with a six-person crew, and the head chef was friendly. I showed up at 3 p.m. and watched as they served up canned artichokes stuffed with instant mashed potatoes and lime-green Jell-O layered with hard-boiled eggs, peas and oysters. I would never serve meals like these.

In the middle of the shift, the fry cook was gone. There was no trout, no oysters, no redfish, nothing. The place was busy and the orders backed up. I walked behind the line and found a man cuddled up around the fryer with an empty vodka bottle, sleeping. I left him there and fried a bunch of seafood. Then all of a sudden a big gong sounded, hurting my ears. What was it? Every time the Cornish game hen was served, a waiter stuck a sparkler in its rear, lit it, hit the gong, and took it to the table. I decided to take a few weeks off from the restaurant business.

I needed a good chef. I needed to really learn. After searching for about a week, I found Daniel Bonnot, the thin, young French chef, often surrounded by adoring women, who ran the four-star Louis XVI hotel and restaurant. Some serious cooking was performed at Louis XVI. French-style waiters served food on silver trays, and vegetables—from eight-sided potatoes to carrots—where precisely cut to uniform size.

Daniel took advantage of my desire to learn. My salary was $40 a day, which ended up being less than $4 an hour because I worked noon to midnight six days a week. All I kept thinking was that the experience was an investment in my future. Someday, it would pay off. I didn't have time to spend my pittance anyway. Luckily there was a laundromat and Chinese restaurant across the street, for something to do if I ever got a day off. A very nice Vietnamese couple did vegetable prep at Louis XVI. They were always astonished at how much waste the restaurant generated, the scraps of food we threw away. In French cooking, many times just the best part of a product is used. The Vietnamese couple offered to save up Saturday night's food scraps and invited me to their house for an early Sunday supper. It was quite a feast.

Paul Prudhomme, meanwhile, had left Commander's Palace to open up his own restaurant, K-Paul's. My roommate, Frank, was the chef there. On my night off, I'd go over to K-Paul's to help Frank out with the strictly Cajun cooking.

At Louis XVI, Chef Daniel was a wild man. He turned out to be worse than Jim Miller, who compared closely to a crabby boot camp sergeant. Nonetheless, the food was fantastic. I learned a great deal about classical preparations, such as rack of lamb en croute, a seared rack painted with a spinach mousse, a compote of wild mushrooms, wrapped in puff pastry, and roasted golden brown. It was garnished with a fresh bouquetiere of vegetables, julienne of carrots, freshly turned potatoes, artichoke bottoms filled with fresh sweet peas, asparagus tips and haricot vert. The lobster américaine was the best. The waiter cooked the lobster in the dining room in fresh whole unsalted butter, shallots, and brandy. The sauce américaine, a crafted classic sauce, was added to the dish.

I started with the rotissiere, butchering all of the beef, veal, ducks and lamb. Then I worked the broiler, cooking all of the meat products. I soon graduated to the saucier station. What a thought: I was a saucier in the French Quarter. It had a nice ring to it. The job entailed fish cutting, oyster preparation and, best of all, creating classic sauces, including hollandaise, bearnaise, Choron, mousseline, américaine and bordelaise, to name a few.

Antoine and Gerhard were the maitre d's at Louis XVI, and they ran the dining room like a precision watch. Service was impeccable. Once while Antoine was in the dining room making bananas Foster—a New Orleans creation with a quickly sautéed glaze over bananas—I was in the back with the dishwashers producing a band concert of glassware, pots and pans and utensils. I still believe that moment was the beginning of rap music. Antoine rushed in, flustered. He had melted his butter and sugar and was ready for the bananas. No bananas.

"Mr. Murray," he said, "we do not run out of bananas."

Being in the French Quarter, I was able to run to the A&P to get bananas. Luckily, Antoine never mentioned this to Chef Daniel. My head would have been on a platter.

Super Bowl Sunday 1980 was the busiest night ever at Louis XVI. One waiter walked out with $1,000 in tips, which made me feel great about the $40 a day I was making. Assorted VIPs, from politicians to musicians to starlets, regularly dined at the restaurant. They came for Daniel's food, and the slaves, myself included, would prepare the meals.

New Orleans is a city that loves its food. It loves its chefs. Among popular chefs, there was a great deal of camaraderie. But there also was an undercurrent of animosity between the classical French school, like Daniel Bonnot, and local or American chefs, like Paul Prudhomme. One day at Louis XVI, I came in early as usual around 11 a.m. I had to prep a couple veal legs, butcher some ducks and French a lot of lamb racks. Chef Daniel walked in about 1 p.m. and I was beaming, nearly finished.

"Hi chef!" I said.

"What is wrong with you?" he bellowed, looking at scraps. "What is that stuff on the floor? You stupid Americans know nothing."

I was shattered.

"Well chef," I finally said, "if we're so stupid, why are you here?"

"Well Phil, the money is really good."

I was determined not to let this wild man get to me. After a year and a half, I mastered the saucier and broiler; I was the best pommes souffle maker there was. I was working elegant parties serving up exquisite classic dishes. And I was still learning a great deal.

During the middle of my second year, I got promoted to sous chef. My pay increased to $50 a day and I had still more hours to put in. I was getting in shape, running five miles a day. I loved life. I would come in at 1 p.m. and got in the habit of drinking the breakfast crew's fresh orange juice. It was really good. Then one night I got sick. I could not stay out of the bathroom and stayed in bed for two days. It was horrible. When I returned, Daniel was actually glad to see me. He said hello.

"Had any orange juice lately?" someone asked me later.

"No."

The staff burst into laughter. They had laced the last batch of orange juice with ex-lax. Just for me. I never touched their orange juice again.

The next week, Daniel invited me to his house for brunch. My goodness, I thought, I've made it. We are buddies. When I arrived, most of the staff and some of Daniel's friends were already there. We ate a good meal, talked and enjoyed ourselves. When it came time to go, I thanked Daniel graciously and headed off to work. I was a few minutes late. What the heck? I was at the boss's house.

As I drove, Daniel dashed past me in his turbo diesel Mercedes at seventy-five miles per hour. What was his hurry? When I arrived at work he was waiting for me.

"Why are you late?" he demanded. "If you want to be a sous chef, you be here on time. How dare you!"

Daniel could make some flawless meals, however. I especially loved his guinea hen Souvoroff. The hens arrived whole and I'd spend six hours plucking feathers, with Daniel coming around every fifteen minutes to check on the progress. We held the birds over open flame to burn off stubborn feathers. Then Daniel seared the whole bird in a large frying pan for a minute or two. He placed them in a large soup tureen, added brandy, fresh-diced black French truffles and fresh foie gras, or goose liver, and then he covered and pasted the lid with salt dough. It baked for about fifty minutes. When Daniel opened the lid, the aroma was so intense, so wonderful, like a magic potion that spread through the air. The scent put the whole staff in a wonderful mood. To serve the guinea hen, Daniel carved off the breast meat and ladled the rich gravy, with truffles and foie gras, over the breasts. It was one of the most memorable food moments of my life.

Soon after all this, I met my future wife, Marilyn, who then was working at a New Orleans hospital training new employees. We met at the 4141 club on Charles Avenue. I walked up to Marilyn's roommate, Micheline Cazayoux, wearing a new Calvin Klein tweed jacket.

"You talk funny," Micheline told me in her New Orleans drawl. "Why don't you go talk to her." She pointed toward Marilyn, a Midwesterner like me. I introduced myself as "Hollingsworth" and told Marilyn that I was from upscale Grosse Pointe, Michigan.

On one of our first dates, Marilyn and I went to a dinner party hosted by an older gentleman named Jay, an apprentice at Louis XVI and a retired real estate agent. The food was good; the company was happy and fun. When I dropped Marilyn off, I coasted toward her house. I wanted to ask her out again. When we started rolling past her house, I graciously opened my car door and used my foot to stop the car. I acted like it was normal. Marilyn agreed to see me again.

Soon after, I began sending her poems, flowers and Perrier Joet champagne. She says she realized my passion—obsession?—for food on a balmy spring New Orleans night when I met her on a ledge outside her apartment at 3:30 a.m., just after getting out of work at Louis XVI. I was teared up because I'd had to cook with frozen chicken. Marilyn just stared at me.

After about a year at Louis XVI, Daniel started to treat me as if I was human. He invited me to enter a professional culinary arts salon, a big show that provided a chance to show off my expertise. I worked after hours on my project, processing, molding, and creating six birdcages made of pastillage, a hard sugary creation. Inside each cage was a pastille dove. The composition was garnished by two chocolate cakes with Victorian-style decorations. The pièce de résistance was a hand-carved chocolate nude, modeled after Marilyn, for the center.

After six weeks of intense work I finished the night before the show. I was excited, hoping to impress my boss and peers, including Paul Prudhomme, who was a judge. Thousands of people were coming. I set up the cakes, birdcages, and statue. Everything looked perfect. It was another hour until judging, so I took a break and began browsing creations by chefs from around the country. About ten minutes before judging, my sculpture got weak and buckled. She landed headfirst in the cake. I ended up with an honorable mention and a vow to never go to a food show again.

After that episode I had another vision about food: I would try to create the best food I could and serve it to guests as soon as possible. That has been much my philosophy on food ever since.

Through the middle of my second year at Louis XVI restaurant, which was inside the Marie Antoinette hotel, Daniel and the hotel's owner bought the ultra-luxury St. Louis Hotel. This French Quarter hotel was filled with period pieces, and I half expected Napoleon Bonaparte to come walking through the door any second. Because of this European atmosphere, a new chef was brought in from France. When Jean Louis showed up, there was a great deal of hoopla.

Jean Louis, a paunched middle-age man, who was a legend in his own mind, traveled with an entourage of three or four people, similar to a rock star. When he walked through our kitchen it was as if the Red Sea split. Introductions were made.

"Jean Louis, this is Phil Murray."

I received the smallest nod from Jean Louis. I was, of course, a stupid American.

In the six weeks before the St. Louis Hotel opened for business, Jean Louis used our kitchen at Louis XVI as his laboratory. At first, small crowds gathered to watch him dice an onion, similar to how people watch Tiger Woods load tees into his golf bag. As days wore into weeks, Jean Louis expressed how he thought our food was bastardized and lousy. Jean Louis would work about half a day and rail at everyone in French. He ate at Louis XVI every night with his friends, always asking for something different and special. Chef Daniel ran around like crazy to make it happen.

Then things got worse. Jean Louis would come in during the day and peek into the walk-in refrigerators and food prep areas, apparently looking to see what we did and didn't have in stock. He then would arrive for dinner and order six côte du bouef à la Provençal—an entrée that inspired Windows' caveman-cut prime rib—knowing full well we only had four in stock. The kitchen, of course, went into a frenzy at his requests. In time, when the staff saw Jean Louis walk in, we'd put our heads down and keep working to avoid being scorned, ignored or passed by as if invisible.

Meanwhile, the St. Louis hotel dining room was still being extensively refurbished. When it was nearly finished, Jean Louis decided that the new ceiling would clash with food, and so the owners tore it down. They spent $20,000 for a new ceiling. When the kitchen was finally completed, Jean Louis and a few members of the Louis XVI staff moved in. I was half hoping to go along because Jean Louis had great talent and I could have learned so much. But what a price.

I was invited for a pre-opening tasting at the St. Louis, and Marilyn came along. We were really excited. It ended up being one of our most memorable dinners ever. The first course was a crawfish appetizer, a salt dough wheelbarrow pushed by an upright crawfish surrounded by a chain-link potato fence garnished with white asparagus.

"Canned white asparagus," I said.

Marilyn shook her head. "It's fresh," she said. "They wouldn't use canned vegetables."

"I'll bet you a bottle of Perrier Joet champagne that it's canned."

Since were were only still dating, I thought it was a good bet. I asked the waiter, and it was true: They had used canned white asparagus. Boy, was that champagne good.

The next course was a fancy caviar and crêpe dish—a $65 appetizer. When it arrived, I could not help but notice that the crêpe was burnt, and I sent it back to the kitchen. What a fatal mistake. Little did I know how incensed Jean Louis would become. I was having a merry time, laughing and giggling and having the time of my life, when I looked up and there, standing in front of me, was Jean Louis.

Jean Louis did not speak much English, so he brought his interpreter with him. Jean Louis started yelling at me in French, fast and furiously. Even his translator had trouble keeping up. While waiting for the translator to speak, I began to feel queasy. The entire dining room stopped talking and eating and all eyes were on our table. After five minutes of yelling, Jean Louis stopped. The translator had one question.

"Why did you send back the crepe?"

Seven words. Translated out of five minutes of intense French ranting. Jean Louis looked like he wanted to kill me.

"It was burnt and I sent it back," I replied.

Jean Louis launched into another tirade while I sat helpless. His face was sweating and nearly purple, and veins were popping out in his forehead and temples. I waited for the barrage to end, and finally the interpreter spoke again.

"Jean Louis wants you to go back in the kitchen and make him a crepe."

I was mad. This guy was totally nuts. There I was, defending myself in English.

"He demands again that you go back in the kitchen and make him a crepe," the interpreter repeated.

"Not now," I yelled back. "But I'll be back at 9 a.m. to make him one."

Plenty of jokes were made about this incident, and I took a great deal of harassment. About eight weeks later, Marilyn and I took a riverboat cruise to listen to a blues band and enjoy a nice evening out. After the band's first set, a small group of people nearby were talking, staring and pointing at me. Some of them were laughing. Was my zipper down? What was going on? One of the women walked toward me.

"Are you the guy who sent the crepe back?"

Later, Jean Louis was caught putting a load of lobster into his car trunk and was fired. Last I heard, he moved to New York City to work his culinary magic.

Back at Louis XVI, Daniel decided to throw another brunch, this time at a friend's restaurant across Lake Pontchartrain, in the small town Slidell. The chef was a polite and cordial Greek gentleman with a classic French bistro-style restaurant. The food was impeccable and creative, and the service was excellent. The chef answered all our questions and was very informative about his food, but all the while I kept my eye on the clock. It was a forty-minute ride back to the French Quarter, and I wasn't about to be late again considering the possible dire consequences from Daniel. When we were nearly finished, the Greek chef received a phone call. We were all happy and jovial, enjoying the excursion. Then we heard a thundering, cantankerous bellowing coming from the Greek chef.

"What do you mean you're sick? Either you're dead or alive! Now get in to work. Right away!"

I was ready to go. Marilyn and I started talking about marriage and we decided we didn't want to spend another hot summer in New Orleans. I told Daniel I planned to leave in three months. They told me I had to leave in two weeks, that my heart and soul wouldn't be in my work if I was leaving.

I needed another job to tide me over for six weeks until Marilyn and I hit the road. A grocery store hired me to butcher meat, and I figured I could use the experience. A crabby butcher showed me all the retail cuts and after three weeks,

I was allowed to butcher a short loin and make T-bones and porterhouses. I cut the wrong direction and was promptly dismissed.

Marilyn and I took an extended vacation after leaving New Orleans. We visited her sister, Martha, in Texas, headed to the Ozark Mountains to camp and fish bass, and traveled to Michigan to see family and friends. There, I interviewed for an exciting-sounding position at a private club in Alaska. The club's headquarters were in Detroit, and the executive in charge wanted to hire me on the spot. I almost said yes. Then he said I'd have to train two years in Detroit. I declined.

We returned to the road and headed north through Petoskey and Sault Ste. Marie, Michigan, before winding through Canada to Toronto and Montreal. Along the way we ate at fine restaurants and gathered ideas for our future. We camped outside beautiful Bangor, Maine, and traveled on to Boston, where we met up with Gaines, my friend from Commander's Palace. After some serious tugging, Marilyn and I decided to get married. Gaines was best man and Marilyn's friend, Jamie, was maid of honor. We had a small wedding, seven guests in all, and spent the next week at Cape Cod.

We were running out of funds, I realized, and I needed a job. Marilyn and I headed to North Carolina where I interviewed for a chain of mid-range restaurants. But I wanted something more challenging. We crawled back northward and found a place in Bowie, Maryland, called Prince George's Country Club. They assured me that I would have free reign in their kitchen.

Jack Nicklaus had designed the course at George's, a club with upscale lodge decor that attracted an upper middle-class clientele. Andy, the sous chef, was the ex-chief petty officer for the *U.S.S. Nimitz*. He claimed to have fed 6,500 people three times a day, seven days a week. I reminded Andy that George's was small—seventy seats—and we were going to cook some nice cuisine. On one of my days off, Andy ordered ten cases of beef tenderloin and fifteen cases of iceberg lettuce.

"Why so much food?" I asked.

"It was on sale," he said.

Soon, I learned that Jack Nicklaus was coming to the club. I wanted to impress him and his entourage. No dice. All Big Jack wanted was tuna fish triangles brought along in the golf cart. To top it off, Big Jack sent back the sandwiches to have the crusts cut off.

Just when I realized the George's job was going nowhere, I received a mysterious call from a man named Lenny. He talked of great riches at his restaurant in downtown Washington, D.C. This former bar owner looked like an older Mel Brooks, and he talked of creating a gourmet restaurant. I was going to be the chef. Meanwhile, as plans moved forward, I worked at Lenny's existing restaurant. We served 200 deli and seafood-special lunches a day, Monday through Friday, followed by a chicken-wing happy hour, then dinner, which didn't draw crowds. From 7 p.m. to 9 p.m., I stood around doing nothing. Or I'd be chopping cabbage while Lenny mixed a gallon of white wine with three ounces of red to make a rosé. Lenny walked in the kitchen one day with this new product called "sea legs"—a seafood hot dog made of processed pollock scraps.

"This is the new appetizer on our menu," he said. "Just microwave it."

I refused to serve sea legs. He next came up with the deviled eggs idea.

"What if we gave one to everybody who came in?"

I was soon gone. Bilbo Baggins was a casual Italian café located in a converted 100-year-old Alexandria, Virginia, townhouse. I'd never worked in such a small kitchen. There was room for two people, me and a helper. Nonetheless, the menu was superb: tempuras, pasta with white clam sauce, curried crab salad with avocado, hearty European-style loaves. The owner was a chef himself, but he was an absentee owner so I had run of the kitchen. I brought all my New Orleans energy to the job and created popular specials like barbecued shrimp, pan-fried redfish and salmon with artichokes and mushrooms. My first child, a son, Nicholas—the namesake of Windows' specialty, tournedo Nicholas—was born while I worked at Bilbo Baggins.

One day I walked around the corner to borrow some carrots from an upscale

French restaurant called Le Bergerie. The chef, a warm, soft-spoken Basque man named John Campagne, told me he was looking for a sous chef and offered to double my current salary. Thrilled, I took a copy of Le Bergerie's menu to study. It consisted of traditional French cooking and specialties from the Basque region of France, including stewed sauces and small, lightly sautéed seafood medallions. My boss at Bilbo Baggins was furious when he learned about my contact with Le Bergerie.

I walked around the corner again and started work at Le Bergerie, an elegant restaurant with circular booths where the chef's brother, Bernard, served as maitre d'. The hours were taxing: six days a week from 9:30 a.m. to 2:30 p.m. then again from 4:30 p.m. to 11:30 p.m. But boy was John good! I felt like I was in culinary school again. John's food and presentation were five star, and the skills I learned at Le Bergerie still strongly influence my dishes today. Chef John's seafood preparations—pepperade of sea scallops, bouillabaisse, sautéed rockfish Basquaise—were exquisite. The confit of pork and ducks and house-made pâtés were divine. The light and robust sauces were made from scratch. Le Bergerie carried only a two-day supply of food and the entrées were cooked in the kitchen and served to guests immediately. This was one of the most organized, consistent, efficient kitchens I had ever worked in.

The only hardship was language. Everyone in the kitchen spoke Spanish. The chef used French terms for food products and Spanish terms to talk about preparation techniques, tools and implements. I occasionally was lost in words. But John was patient with me. He took his time and listened and explained. Of all the restaurant owners and chefs I've ever worked with, he was the kindest and most loving. I learned more at Le Bergerie in a year than I did anyplace else.

But, as with Commander's Palace, I reached a point after about a year where I had learned all I could. My career demanded new challenges.

When I found out about a new French Creole restaurant opening up in downtown Washington, D.C., in 1983, I was all ears. I was ready. Chef John agreed it was time for me to move on. He helped me with the cooking interview so I was able to use volutes, stocks, and garnishes.

Lafitte was located inside the intimate four-star Hampshire Hotel just south of Dupont Circle. I went through a series of interviews with Leo, the district manager, and prepared some Creole and Cajun specialties that were textbook masterpieces. Chef John at Le Bergerie allowed me to use his kitchen to prep garnishes and sauces before meeting with Leo. During the third interview, Leo laid out the corporate spiel. I was amazed at the company's reach. They had numerous hotels and gourmet restaurants in India, the Middle East, London and elsewhere. Lafitte would be their first foray into the United States. They wanted a Creole showplace. I gladly accepted the position.

Lafitte had already been designed. The dining room contained art deco details and mirrors on the walls and ceiling. Tables were topped with exotic flowers and bottles of Tabasco sauce. The kitchen, however, was poorly and inefficiently designed. Working there was going be stressful. But, as Leo would say, "Hally Ho!" I had negotiated a one-week trip to New Orleans to obtain food supplier information. It also was a much-needed vacation. I called in every day to report my business doings and tried to sound like I was drudging along New Orleans's streets, hard at work. But it was Mardi Gras, and I still can picture my son Nicholas bouncing up and down in his backpack, hooked to my dancing wife, Marilyn.

When we returned, I ordered equipment needed to run a good kitchen, including a $16,000 European Master Bakers stove. Leo won't mind, I thought. I put finishing touches on the menu. It was going to be good. I could feel it. In two weeks, Lafitte was scheduled to open and I was busy testing recipes, doing tastings and ordering china. On the day my first equipment order arrived—including stock pots, brazier pots, a salmon poacher—the manager, a Mr. Stephen Goodchild, an Englishman right from London, came to see me. It was most urgent.

"You're way over budget," this polished and well-mannered gentleman said.

I had spent approximately $22,000 and the kitchen's budget was $1,100. He said I couldn't buy anything else.

"Well, you tell Leo that I cannot do this kind of food without the proper equipment!"

That is where the war started. Leo wanted to achieve the largest return on the smallest investment known to the business world. There was no way I could possibly prepare the caliber of food they wanted without proper tools and equipment. I called Leo. After about fifteen minutes on the phone, I was back in business.

Splendid Stephen always took a neutral stance when it came to me fighting with Leo to get investments made in the kitchen. Stephen was a friendly, courteous, and well-trained restaurant manager whose charm could make someone feel honored to receive a burnt dinner. His politeness and civility surprised me much of the time. My gruff and rough-around-the-edges personality also was a constant shocker to Stephen. But he was impressed with the food and we worked hard together for a nice product.

The help at Lafitte's was mostly inexperienced, but they were all positive and hard workers. There was Christo, Rocky, Raphael and Jose 1, the Latin version of Charles Bronson. One morning Jose was late. It wasn't normal for Jose 1 to be late, ever. Jose 1 was the head dishwasher and the security man. He would not let anyone in the kitchen without an appointment, something he'd tell them most often while tapping a knife on the counter. A skinny man walked up to me.

"I Jose 2."

"Where is Jose?" I asked.

"I Jose 2, Jose 1 in jail."

"All right, you're on the dishes," I said.

Jose 2 worked the lunch shift. As the dishes started coming in, Jose 2 started furiously eating the plate scraps. My goodness, I thought, this guy is starving. I wondered when he had his last meal. But Jose 2 was a hustler and he caught on in no time. I enrolled him in the health care plan and paid him as much as possible. In no time at all, these guys were doing great work.

I was getting used to combining French, Spanish, and English. I'd point at a food product and Rocky, Christo, and Raphael would tell me what it was. While actually doing prep or presentation work, the staff caught on quickly. Still, we didn't communicate fluently, just enough to get by using code words. It was pretty quiet during busy times because everyone was watching, listening, and learning.

Little did I realize that Cajun and Creole food would become the rage. People phoned in daily to ask when we were opening. The pressure and stress mounted. When we finally opened, I started with breakfast and worked all the way through dinner. I had carte blanche in the kitchen, but was lucky to have them close on Sunday so I could have a day off. Lafitte got busier daily. I had produced an eclectic mix of French Creole specialties mixed with Basque and classic French preparations. All of the positive response I received was fuel for me to work like a wild banshee. We made everything from scratch, from ice cream to bread to entrées.

After about a month we were booked a week in advance. When dinner sold out, the lunch crowd grew. I was frantic and enjoying every minute. Food supplies were gone the same day they came in. It was unbelievable. President Reagan's daughter, Maureen, liked the Chicken Boursin at Lafitte. She would bring a friend in for dinner and order two salads and two Chicken Boursins. Meanwhile, the four Secret Service agents always ordered healthy courses, often the most expensive items on the menu. I still wonder where my tax dollars go.

I made an appointment with Leo to ask for a raise, thinking he would understand and pay me what I was really worth. Instead, I heard the "maybe, possibly" routine about opening a Creole restaurant in London—"a real opportunity"—instead of a raise.

I showed up at 7 a.m. and finished at midnight. I wasn't sleeping. I knew I couldn't continue at such a pace. Then it dawned on me: I could hire a pastry chef, a sous chef and some more cooks. Leo was just getting over the financial bruising of the equipment and I figured it was time to see if he was ready to grow more gray hair. But I knew that our profit margins were stunning. Lafitte's labor costs took up only fifteen percent of gross—compared to a typical twenty-five to thirty percent in restaurants. Meanwhile, food costs were at only thirty percent, rather than a more usual forty percent.

Leo was playing me for a fool. I had saved him thousands in labor by doing everything. Well, I figured I could cut back my hours and have more time at home. So instead of getting a raise I'd get a complete staff and wouldn't have to worry about working 100-hour weeks anymore. Within a week I had more staff. Mickey Cannon, a talented chef from Pittsburgh, Pennsylvania, came aboard and proved a godsend. We saw eye-to-eye about food. I thought Leo was going to have a fit with the added payroll, but by the end of the month, sales were stronger than ever. The restaurant just kept getting busier. The locals from Washington, D.C. and the suburbs were flocking to us.

Rumor had it that Lafitte was going to be reviewed by *The Washington Post* Magazine's Phyllis Richman, who had a reputation of making and breaking restaurants. She had a considerable following and her word of acceptance was a good omen. As weeks passed, I watched the Sunday paper for Richman's column. Four weeks in a row, she trashed restaurants in her nit picky, truthful, and honest reviews. I began hoping she would skip us. We were already doing great business and people loved the food. I finally received a call from *The Washington Post* alerting us that the review was being published on July 15, 1984.

"Is it positive?" I asked.

"Well, you have to wait and see on Sunday."

I was shaking in my boots. This was make-it or break-it time.

"For Washington," Richman wrote, "Lafitte is a change of taste. This is gutsy cooking, with seasonings that draw your attention and stay in your memory."

The lengthy review applauded the interesting choices of à la carte vegetables, called the duck Dumaine succulent and outstanding, and said Lafitte was the first "of what we hope is a trend." Richman told readers to investigate the pastry cart and advised: "Above all, reserve a piece of the chocolate raspberry torte, which is dense, buttery, fudgy and intensely rich, saved from being cloying by the tart, fresh berries. It is a spectacular bit of chocolate cookery."

We were hot. Now was the time to hit Leo for a raise.

"Congratulations Phil, nice job," Leo said after reading the review.

"Well how about a raise?"

"Let me put it is this way, your costs are not within the budget and your salary is above budget and the hotel occupancy rate is two percent under budget," he said. "We have to tighten our belts and work a little harder, and by the way the CEO of the company is coming from India to visit. We need to get everything in shape for the big visit."

I figured if I could really impress the big cheese and land a position in Europe somewhere, it would be worth sweating it out. The next week was hell. Leo came into the kitchen to bug me every day: What could we cut? How could we save more money? What was I going to do? All I could say is that the place was booming and we were surpassing our sales goals, the kitchen was spotless and sanitary, and we were making great food.

"Still Phil, we need to cut costs. We need to have more profit."

I was getting tired of Leo.

When the big day arrived, we were all in our dress whites. Everything was impeccable. We were prepared to make the big shots a lunch so top notch that they wouldn't forget it. Leo brought them through the kitchen and made introductions, and then the corporate executives went out to be seated. Leo reappeared carrying two large Styrofoam to-go containers filled with green peas and yellow vegetables. He handed it to me. It was carry-out from a local Indian restaurant.

"Heat it up and serve it to the big cheese," Leo instructed. "He is a vegetarian."

I was crushed. I refused to serve the carry-out. Someone else heated it up. That was the last straw. I was being compromised by Leo again and I was ready to move on.

Marilyn, meanwhile, had begun working in restaurants. Eating out had always been one of her favorite pastimes, and she wanted to keep the same schedule as me. When she was pregnant with Nicholas, she waited tables at La Colline on Capital Hill in Washington, D.C., which served a bouillabaisse that inspired the recipe now used at Windows. Marilyn served such notables as Ted Kennedy and other politicians and, during split shifts while pregnant, she'd nap on the capital lawn near the lit dome. Later, as we began talking about going into business ourselves, Marilyn took a bookkeeping job at Evan's Farm Inn in McLean, Virginia.

I, meanwhile, had been getting offers for other jobs. I mostly brushed them off but now was ready to take a plunge—where, I didn't know. One night, a regular customer came in and asked if I would be interested in opening a country inn in Middleburgh, Virginia, and the prospect set off another round of excitement. I was ready to start over. I would be part owner. We went back and forth, visited the site, which was a beautiful piece of property, an old plantation, but was dilapidated and needed total renovation. The money guys seemed tight on the deal and I soon lost interest after Marilyn and I visited Traverse City on vacation and got a bug to explore northern Michigan.

We headed back to Michigan in the summer of 1985 to sort out our options and get some rest and relaxation. We visited friends and family in Detroit, and Marilyn suggested going up to Traverse City to see an old college friend. John and Ann Marie Mitchell lived in Suttons Bay, a small, quaint lakeside village about twelve miles north of Traverse City. My first impression of the area was that it was small, protected, and that locals treated outsiders as, well, outsiders. Trying to break the ice with John Mitchell was like trying to pry open a fresh clam with bare fingers.

Ann Marie was cordial and helpful, and she recommended we try some of the region's top restaurants during our three-night stay. The food was very good, but I knew I could do just as good or better. During our last day, Marilyn and I walked the beach for a long time. What about finding a restaurant up here? Was it feasible? We decided to revisit my old culinary school at Schoolcraft College to gather information about the Traverse City area. I was ready to commit, optimistic, just praying that somehow this would work out.

When I walked back into school ten years later the place had doubled in size.

There were new chefs everywhere. Luckily, Mr. Breithaupt, the executive chef in charge, was still there. I talked fast and excitedly to him, and Breithaupt was helpful, but doubted our fantasy because of Traverse City's small size. Nonetheless, he gave me a restaurant broker's phone number.

When we returned to Washington, I called and described our dream of opening a gourmet restaurant in northern Michigan.

"First of all," the broker said, "do you have any money?"

"Sure, we have plenty."

Actually we had none. But we had plenty of equity in our home, and I was planning to use that for a down payment. Two weeks later he called back. There were two operating restaurants for sale in the area. I was jumping with joy.

"When can you come to take a look around?"

I managed to talk to Leo and arrange a few days off without letting the cat out of the bag. We flew back to Detroit; the brokers picked us up for the four-hour drive to Traverse. The first restaurant was on Front and Division streets, a busy intersection in Traverse City, the hub of northern Michigan's tourist and cherry-growing country. Gas stations were on the other three corners. I loved the place. Our location did not matter. The food was going to be the best, and the people would come. My mind was made up: I wanted the place. That was that. Marilyn was a little more patient.

"Let's not make any decisions quite yet," she said.

As we traveled up along West Grand Traverse Bay's shoreline, all I could think about was that restaurant. I had already settled into the kitchen. All I needed was some minor equipment to get started. We pulled up to the second restaurant on M-22 called Leone's Pier 22, I was unimpressed. It looked like a bar off Eight Mile Road in Detroit. But when we walked in and I saw all of the windows—hence the name—I forgot all about that other restaurant. The view of the bay and nearby peninsula and islands was beautiful. I figured the place was probably out of our price range.

The owner, Don Leone, was tinkering around the place, working on wiring, and he immediately began chatting about the restaurant, its clientele, his experience there. His wife, Peg, was in the kitchen. She took me aside and said that Don was ready to retire. His knees were getting bad. Within fifteen minutes we told Don Leone we wanted to buy the restaurant. Nothing was said about the price. We just fell in love with the place and we were determined to make a go of it.

It worked in our favor that the broker had told Don Leone we had a boatload of cash and were ready to buy. Of course, we had only a shoebox full. I was so excited I could barely contain myself. Pier 22 was a well-kept place, with only minimal work needed.

We were on our way. But we didn't know how much the restaurant would cost. Could we afford it? There were so many details. Could this work? Was this just a pipe dream? We had to wait and see. We headed back to Washington.

The broker called and said Don Leone wanted cash for everything. We were dead. What about a land contract? The broker was apprehensive and felt we were fishing, didn't have any cash and were wasting his time. I finally called Don Leone and talked to him directly, asking him for financial details, such as sales tax receipts and other information.

"By the way, could you sell us the restaurant cheaper?" I asked. "Would you consider a land contract? Could you? Please?"

Don Leone sensed our urgency and commitment.

"I'll get back with you," he said.

This was not going to work. We did not have enough cash. The broker phoned. They wanted $100,000 down. We could rent the property and pay taxes and insurance and we would be buying the business and liquor license and so forth. We were sunk. We did not have that kind of money. There was no way. I was devastated. I kept putting figures together, but it was useless.

I called Don Leone to tell him we could not afford it. He replied within ten seconds.

"Would a much smaller down payment be OK?" he asked. "You could make up the remainder of the deposit in the next couple years."

"Yes, yes, yes," I said.

We sent out a $5,000 deposit in September 1985. We were on our way.

I was ready to tell Leo. I couldn't wait. He didn't know what had been going on in Michigan and thought I was going to grovel for another raise. As I started talking, he started getting the gist of my plans and interrupted first with an offer for a paltry five-percent raise. Then he offered me a move to England to open a new hotel.

"I could put you over there, but there would be a pay cut, and your family would have to pay themselves to go over."

"Is that all you have to offer Leo?"

"How are you going to pay for the restaurant?"

I told him my financial plan. He laughed.

"You'll never make it on your own. You'll be out of business in a month."

"Maybe, but it'll be a month of my life that I'll never forget."

I thanked Leo and officially gave my thirty-day notice. We put our house up for sale and started networking in northern Michigan. One evening I received a call from an energetic real estate agent named Jim Stacy.

"Hey, how ya doing? Looking to buy a house? We have a lot on the market right now."

It was starting all ready. Jim Stacy ended up being a dear friend and confidante, along with his wife, Becky, who worked at Windows as a waitress. Near the end of our stay in Washington, I received a call asking if I could consult for a month for $10,000. I taught an Iranian chef and Moroccan maitre d' how to cook Cajun food. The pair almost drove me into the loony bin.

When we first arrived in Traverse City, I was really scared. We were putting everything on the line. We were attempting, with great passion, to open a high-caliber restaurant unlike any in the region, to bring fine dining to our part of northern Michigan. Marilyn said she knew, no matter what happened, we could not quit, could not give up, and it was that resolve that saw us through our difficult early years.

We arrived in January, so there was time to get things rolling before the busy summer season. We met with an attorney and accountant, and each warned us about the food business. Restaurants have a seventy percent failure rate, they said, and to go into business with your wife compounds the failure rate. We weren't deterred. They were all crazy. They didn't know a thing about the restaurant business.

We went out to eat several times with our Suttons Bay friends, John and Ann Marie Mitchell. We visited the acclaimed Bluebird in Leland, along Lake Michigan's west shore. Another night we ate at Epicure in Suttons Bay, where John was a regular customer. He asked the chef to prepare us something special. I felt like I was out of my league. That is, until I received my food. Then I knew we had a chance. We invited the Mitchells to dinner. I figured it would give us a chance to understand and get to know each other better. Plus, I was getting itchy to cook for someone.

For dinner, I selected some smoked food I was thinking of including on Windows' menus: frog legs, shrimp, salmon. I was confident that this dinner would break the ice. The frog legs turned out so rubbery and salty they weren't edible. The shrimp and salmon were horrible. John Mitchell did not say much. He did not eat much either. Matter of fact, he spent the next fourteen years reminding me of that infamous chewy frog leg dinner.

As each day rolled closer to our closing date, I would visit Don Leone and learn something new about the restaurant, mostly maintenance tips. He tried to tell me about the food people liked in northern Michigan and what his clientele liked. I did not listen.

When we closed the deal on March 3, I was to buy his existing inventory, foods, wine, beer everything. No big deal. One night at 3 a.m. I woke up and realized that I was going to buy this guy's leftover food—frozen lobster tails, frozen fried chicken, other foodstuffs. I dressed in a panic the next day, rushed over and told him I didn't want any food at all.

"Son, you signed a contract. You have to buy all the food," he said.

"Well, please try to keep your inventory down."

I kept bugging him until the final three days he was open. We would close the deal on Wednesday and reopen on Friday. We had two days to get together a menu and retrain existing staff. On closing day, I ended up buying very little food, only one lobster tail, eight shrimp, a block of cheddar cheese and some lettuce.

I drove three hours to Lansing to switch over the liquor license. I waited an hour in line. The clerk said the paperwork wasn't in order. I headed home to our lawyer's office. After he fixed the papers, I headed back downstate and waited in line. Another clerk said the application wasn't properly filled out. I'd have to come back. I sat down and, for two hours, completed the application and picked up my license.

Heading back to Traverse, I was nervous. Friends from my years in restaurants, however, had heroically arrived to help launch the venture. Steve, my friend from years back at Leopold Bloom's in Ann Arbor, had come aboard at Windows and, when I returned from Lansing, he was in the kitchen doing prep work with a couple other helpers. Mickey Cannon, the Pittsburgh chef with whom I'd worked at Lafitte, also stepped in. Marilyn's roommate from New Orleans, Micheline Cazayoux, arrived to wait tables that summer.

Marilyn hand wrote the menu, which included six to eight items priced between $6.95 and $12.95. We worried that the high prices might scare off customers. We were really tight on money. We needed to open on Friday. We needed to get some cash flow going.

Windows restaurant opened March 3, 1986. I had spent twelve years working in the trenches, honing my craft in various restaurants. The week before we opened, I thought I was going to die. How could I take all of our savings and talk my wife into going into business? My side hurt, my teeth ached, and I was a nervous wreck. I went to the doctor to find that I had a kidney stone and that it would pass in time.

Our first night was a nightmare. The old staff did things the Don Leone way, the complete opposite of my method. The clientele were mostly business contacts— accountants, insurance agents, advertising representatives. They didn't bring guests. But they did offer advice: Gee, you need better china. You should remodel the bathrooms. You need different carpet. Why don't you put more flowers out? No one said anything about the food. No one seemed to care, except for Marilyn and me.

Our first night we grossed $1,100. It was the hardest I had worked in my life.

When we opened, we inherited some of Don's dedicated staff. Tim Middaugh, a 15-year-old dishwasher, was the whiz of the kitchen. He had a place for everything, and he was very fast and clean. The second night we were open, he disappeared. I went outside behind the walk-in and found him.

"This is a good way to be fired," I told him. "I really need your help."

"Sure, I'll help you," Tim replied.

We couldn't have made it through the summer without his efficiency and knowledge of the restaurant. Tim continued to work for Windows for the next six years and is, to this day, a very talented chef and restaurant manager. Cory Luna, the son of our nanny, also started working at the restaurant when he was 14 years old. He started as a dishwasher and, in a dozen years, worked all the kitchen stations except sauté before becoming our pastry and garde manger chef.

As those early days wore on and the stress levels grew, criticism increased: The food was okay, people said, but we should do this or that. It was a mess. We were busy the first two nights then we were slow. Was the place that bad? Marilyn faced numerous nightmarish evenings learning to manage the dining room, from scheduling to reservations to teaching servers the fine art of keeping water glasses filled. Tension levels often were high. One evening a lady came in for dinner and asked me how I liked the new restaurant. I told her that I was getting frustrated, almost at my wit's end. This lady proceeded to tell me that there were six restaurants there before me, and every one of them had failed. Great, I thought. I was going to be number seven.

I later learned that Don Leone had bought and sold the restaurant several times.

He would collect a generous deposit and take the property back when the lessee couldn't make payment. What a way to make money. So when the first month's payment was due, I confronted Don Leone about this scenario. By this time, I already felt like we were taken advantage of and the monthly payments and balloon payments were too much. We would surely fail. Don Leone assured us that this was not his intention. He wanted to retire and did not want to get back in the restaurant business. Yes, he took back the restaurant several times, but with all the repairs and reselling he did not make any money. I still was very dubious.

By the beginning of the second month we still had no business. To drum up guests, I actually changed my menu and started serving some food from Don Leone's days: beer battered shrimp, prime rib, cottage fries, and frog legs. I was fighting for my life and we were sinking. I had trouble sleeping. I was dumbfounded. Later, I realized that we had opened up during the off season. During winters, there simply weren't that many people in northern Michigan, a summer-time tourist playground.

Windows became a real work in progress. Don Leone had shown us how to make candles, melting fifty pounds of wax and lining up the wicks. Wax went everywhere and we were getting really frustrated with all the do-it-yourself projects to save a few dollars. It took valuable time, and the kitchen was where I needed to be. It finally dawned on me that I should buy ready-made candles. Then, when things broke, I started calling in professionals—plumbers, electricians—instead of trying to fix it myself. I decided to simply concentrate on the food and leave everything else to the experts.

Eventually, I decided to scrap the menu and go with the items I created. It was time to go for broke. I reworked my menu and went for it. If I was going to fail, I reasoned, it was going to be with the food that I liked to cook, with food that made me proud.

Windows' first two years were the toughest. Marilyn and I had used up all our back-up capital of $25,000 during our first year. The business was running on a day-to-day basis. I kept telling myself over and over: Create the best food and everything else will take care of itself.

In time, the formula began to work. We started getting busier and busier, and as the busines grew, we began taking more chances. New carpet was expensive, but we had three months to pay for it. Then came some new china, wine glasses here, and breadbaskets there. Finally we had a good summer and some cash in the bank.

"Wow," I told myself, "we'll be here next summer."

Midwest dining, especially at Windows, grew mostly from word of mouth. The fact that business was growing meant, to me, that people liked the food and the menu choices. Nonetheless, I kept changing menus. I continually searched to see what other restaurants were offering in Chicago, New York City, San Francisco, New Orleans and Washington, D.C. For a while, I felt I was a step ahead because I occasionally offered new whacked-out nouvelle menu choices: kiwi-garnished raspberry-vinaigrette aardvaark-mousse cuisine.

Among highlights of my cuisine experimentation was Wild Game Night in 1988. I put rattlesnake fritter on the menu. I ordered it from a wild game catalog, and it arrived cryo-vac sealed, looking like a meat-free snake skeleton, a pale fossil with bony marks down it. I took the snake out, simmered it, strained the meat out, mixed it with flour, eggs, and garlic and fried it. The guests hated it: Fried white flour with boiled rattlesnake remnants. The saving grace of the Wild Game Night fiasco was the dessert. I served chocolate burger buddies, which were miniature chocolate macaroons glued together with chocolate ganach to resemble small hamburgers, complete with chopped white chocolate as onions, raspberry sauce as ketchup and pistachio nuts as pickles. The dessert was accompanied by French fries—almond biscuit cake—sitting within a French fry bag made from milk chocolate.

It took me ten years to figure out that if it isn't broke, don't fix it. Our guests kept coming back for the really consistent, delicious dinners we prepared. I finally came to the conclusion that if you take the best possible ingredients and put your soul into it, it's magic.

Windows has a large group of regular customers, some of whom have been with us from day one. They are the backbone of our business. There's an appliance store owner, Mr. Owens, who's come in ten years running, every two weeks, for our duck confit. His lovely wife orders the steamed Norwegian salmon, no butter, with steamed fresh vegetables. Mr. and Mrs. Lewis have been coming in since we opened our doors. Mr. Lewis only orders tournedo Nicholas, and the couple arrives at 5 p.m. sharp. When we see them, we cut his filet and start cooking. May and Doc Ruhman have been instrumental to our success. May ordered the crispy chicken Boursin so many times that we named the dish after her. Whole families regularly dine with us, and summer residents make special trips each year for dinner at Windows with friends. Our collection of crab cake junkies returns repeatedly for what they call the best crab cakes in the Midwest.

After our first full year in business, Marilyn and I decided to throw a Mardi Gras party to thank our devoted customers for their allegiance the previous year. Marilyn had experienced about six Mardi Gras celebrations in New Orleans, while I had been through four. Even our son Nicholas had been part of the revelry. I can still picture him bouncing up and down in his little backpack, hooked to a dancing Marilyn.

We advertised for Windows' first Mardi Gras gala and threw a huge party with a live band, a juggler, balloons, doubloons, costumes, and purple, green and gold decorations—the whole nine yards. The grandiose buffet included plump shrimp, crawfish étouffée, jambalaya, crab legs, and more. The food was, and is, legendary. We set out to overwhelm our guests, and I prepared more than they could possibly eat. They tried to eat it all, but there was always more. Even foul weather didn't deter our Mardi Gras merrymakers. In the winter of 1991, we had a huge blizzard with white-outs and weather advisories. The band was already there, we had a boatload of food, and I had a sinking feeling in my stomach. I had recently had a conversation with our food purveyor.

"I know of more than 100 restaurants that went out of business because of consecutive bad-weather weekends," he'd told me.

I watched the snow falling, certain that our time was up.

Lo and behold, during a major blizzard, everybody showed up for the party. We had record attendance for our Mardi Gras gala. Everyone had a blast. No one cared about the weather. The first Mardi Gras party was the only year we advertised. Each subsequent year has been a complete sell out, and many people now make reservations twelve months in advance. (Look in the following section for a Mardi Gras recipe for 300 guests. Peruse it, mix it together, and have a blast.)

But not all our special events have been a success. Buffets, for instance. I tried twice to stage buffets, once on Sunday afternoons, and I put great energy into the effort. Unfortunately, few people came. I withered. I got depressed. The next year, I tried a nouvelle California whacko-liberal à la carte menu. Again, a flop. My last foray into marketing brunch was for Father's Day: "Dads eat free!" Besides selling Yahoo! stock too early, this was one of my most memorable idiotic ideas. One table, a six-top, included a father, a mother and four grown sons, all of whom claimed to have fathered children. These guests ate about thirty pounds of food and paid $13.95 for the entire meal. The whole day was similar. We fed about 200 people with our fine cuisine and took in about $90 for the day.

After this episode, I took on new leadership qualities with Marilyn and the rest of the staff: "Humor him," they'd say, "but don't let him get away with any more crazy ideas." This eventually translated into: "Let Phil know about nothing until the last resort." This meant keeping me out of the dining room. To keep me from embarrassing anyone and myself, I was told that I belonged in the kitchen and I was going to stay there.

Luckily, Father's Day brunch acquired new meaning at Windows soon after the dads-eat-free incident. Rib-master John Mitchell proposed doing a benefit Father's Day brunch. For the following nine years, John barbecued some phenomenal ribs and I supplied the remainder of the meal. John's ribs alone have attracted a following of their own. We donate the day's proceeds to a local charity.

"I do this to keep you out of Satan's frying pan," John tells me each year.

Windows also serves brunch on Easter and Mother's Day. Together with our Father's Day rib feast, it's about all the brunch we can handle. We've also catered upscale weddings, rehearsal dinners, graduation parties, anniversaries and black-tie retirement gatherings. The rumor around northern Michigan was that if it was at Windows, everyone would show up.

From the time Windows opened in 1986 until 1996, Marilyn handled everything past the coffee machines: the dining room, wait staff, bus staff, bartenders, hosts and wine list. Marilyn ran the dining room like a Swiss watch. All of the guests were personally taken care of and her army of servers was well trained, professionally attired, and extremely competent. Their only problem was Phil the Chef in the Kitchen. Once, during an extremely busy night, a customer sent his dinner back to be re-prepared. Then he sent it back again. When he sent his dinner back a third time, I took off my apron and started to storm into the dining room. I was going to deal with him. A staff member ran out to get Marilyn.

"Marilyn—Phil's coming!"

"Oh no he's not," Marilyn said.

She stood in the doorway to the kitchen, blocking me from leaving, and held her hand up, like a stop sign.

"You're not going anywhere," she told me. "You get back in there and keep cooking."

I took a deep breath and returned to the kitchen. I left the customer relations to her. Marilyn became a pro at handling our biggest customer relations dilemma: Everyone wanted one of the seven tables by the windows. One regular even offered to pay $10,000 for a permanent window-table reservation. But with Marilyn at the helm, most customers ended up feeling good about wherever they were seated.

An invisible line had been drawn between my kitchen and Marilyn's dining room, where she obsessed over the repetition and details that mark service in a fine-dining establishment. She ensured that cocktails were immediately served and water glasses filled, and she taught the wait staff to anticipate customers' needs and deftly come and go from tables without diners even noticing. We were dedicated to high standards.

So dedicated, in fact, that Marilyn even worked feverishly during her pregnancies with our daughters. Marilyn worked the Saturday night prior to the birth of our third child, Gabrielle, in December 1989, squeezing between tables with her mammoth tummy. She said Windows was the world's best grocery store for pregnant women, with ice cream, tomatoes, and olives on demand.

The restaurant's former owner, Don Leone, had joked that he put his kids in boxes while working. Our three children didn't quite get that treatment, but they ended up becoming the youngest gourmet diners in the world. While other children were enchanted by macaroni and cheese, ours grew to love venison, capers, lobster and bouillabaisse. Once, our son, Nicholas went with some friends to Don's Drive-In, a traditional hamburger joint in Traverse City. There, he ordered a raspberry milkshake and a burger with sautéed mushrooms and Swiss cheese. He was five.

The kids also helped out at the restaurant. Marilyn would come to pick up the girls and there they were in big aprons helping make mocha truffles, covered head to toe in chocolate, grinning like there was no tomorrow. When Nicholas was sixteen, he began helping with prep work and dishwashing. With his first paycheck, he brought friends into the restaurant and bought dinner.

In September 1987, the *Detroit News* featured Windows in a living-section cover story titled "Upstate Treats." Writer Sandra Silfven raved about the restaurant's breathtaking views "of gulls playing tag over white-crested waves of the west arm of Grand Traverse Bay."

"Plastic tablecloths and wood paneling may convey a casual menu, but the food of chef-owner Phil Murray is dead serious," she wrote of the atmosphere in the days before we could afford linen tablecloths. The story talked about Windows' upscale menu, saying the cuisine was a "charming American style with savory Cajun and French accents." It mentioned one of Windows' standard dishes, Veal Wynn Dixie, lobster meat with fresh quartered artichoke hearts on escallops of veal in a jalapeño butter sauce.

"It's the desserts, though, where the true heart of the restaurant beats," Silfven summed up. "Murray is a pro with chocolate."

I absolutely love chocolate. I have been eating candy bars and sweets since I was two years old, and for special occasions—Mother's Day, Easter, Christmas, birthdays— I bought my mother boxes of chocolates. I eagerly anticipated her unwrapping the gift and, before she could say "thank you," I would ask for a chocolate. Often, I ate the whole box. My mother also made mean fudge. My siblings and I clamored around her so we could have the spoon or scrape the pan. Throughout the years, I have eaten or tasted every type of chocolate confection produced on this planet. One of my early favorites were Hostess Ding-Dongs. I don't know why. Once, I received a chocolate fruit and nut egg for Easter. I took it outside and slapped it around with a hockey stick until I accidentally shot it through a neighbor's window. All this didn't exactly prime me for chocolate work, but it marked the beginnings of a lifelong devotion to chocolate.

Desserts have been a work in progress at Windows since the restaurant's inception, though when we first opened, it was difficult to find suppliers who carried fine products. Most of my instructors were European chefs who were experienced in handling the finest courverture, or professional-quality chocolate, and who showed me the chocolate's many fine qualities. Much of the mystery surrounding chocolate began with the French, who claim that top cocoa beans are used in Europe and that rejected beans are used in America, especially to make candy bars. To explore this theory, try taste-testing a piece of European chocolate and a piece of American chocolate. There is quite a difference. The aroma, fullness of character, and wholesomeness of European chocolate is divine and remarkable. At Windows, we use some pretty simple dessert recipes, and the difference fine European chocolate makes is evident.

Advances in technology, particularly in refining, have enhanced the purity of flavor in fine chocolate, and new procedures, such as transfer sheets, allow chocolates to be decorated by such things as twenty-four carat gold. At Windows, we have exclusively used Cocoa Barry Chocolates. The staff and I have attended six Cocoa Berry Chocolate classes over the years, where we were tutored by classically trained chocolatiers. This education has helped us create top-quality desserts. We have adapted many recipes to fit our needs.

Mary Boudjalis, a dear friend and a loyal customer, once asked for an assortment of desserts on the menu, and the Windows' pupu platter was born. This outrageous concoction of all of our desserts was the rage. It got so popular it backed up the garde manger station. Our guests stayed an extra hour, on average, devouring desserts. We soon realized it was cutting into our turnover rate and we put an end to the chocolate orgy. Pupu platters are still available, however, upon request for special occasions. A couple once came in and special ordered a pupu platter, which is designed to feed six people. A petite gentleman, who weighed about 160 pounds, ate the entire platter along with his dinner. I couldn't believe my eyes.

Over the years, I have taught a few classes on preparing chocolate and desserts, but I learned I have no patience when it comes to teaching. After some unsuccessful forays into this field, I decided to leave the teaching to teachers. I am better off staying in the kitchen where I belong.

I was determined early on to give each guest, whether they ordered dessert or not, a sampling of our chocolate. We decided to deliver, with every check, a truffle for each diner. Today, some regular customers often skip dessert, knowing that a chocolate delicacy awaits. Our chocolate recipes have evolved and Windows now serves eight time-tested truffle flavors, our guests' favorites. During our four annual buffets—Easter, Mother's Day, Father's Day and Mardi Gras—we serve every kind of chocolate creation known to us. We also sell boxes of chocolates so guests can take truffles home.

When naming desserts, we avoided terms like "chocolate suicide" and "death by chocolate." Chocolate provides a natural euphoria and comfort that can only be found in its wonderful ingredients, and we wanted positive, uplifting names that reflected the magic of chocolate.

When our first daughter, Olivia, was born in 1987, chocolate mousse Olivia also was born. Over the years, this has been our top-selling dessert. I wish I had saved the $6 charged for all the chocolate mousse Olivias sold. I would be driving a Ferrari.

When our second daughter, Gabrielle, was born in 1989, I frantically worked on some dessert specials to name after her. I finally developed the princess Gabrielle, two petite cream puffs, one filled with French vanilla ice cream and the other filled with chocolate raspberry ice cream and raspberry sauce. The wait staff cringed every time a guest ordered one, and eventually I took it off the menu. One day, Gabrielle came into the restaurant and began reading the menu.

"Why is Olivia first?" Gabrielle asked. "Why can't I be first?"

She scanned through the rest of dessert list: Chocolate raspberry torte, northern star, opera cake, pecan cheesecake, creme caramel, mucho mocha, turtle sundae and ice cream cake.

"Hey! Wait a minute," she said. "I'm not on the menu. Mucho Mocha has replaced me. Dad!"

"Sorry Gabrielle."

Windows' ice creams also have been perennial favorites. We take the word ice cream literally, meaning that we use cream, all cream. Our ice cream is not for the calorie counters. The mix of fresh whole cream and chocolate is a taste sensation. Our best-received products include chocolate raspberry, milk chocolate mocha, white chocolate with dried cherries, and French vanilla. Fresh fruit sorbet has been a nice alternative. We use fresh Leelanau strawberries, fresh apricots and cherries, which we serve when the Cherry Queen and her court arrive for their annual dinner during Traverse City's National Cherry Festival.

I have tried more than twenty kinds of cheesecakes and nothing has compared to our pecan cheesecake. We experimented for years and finally gave up and just kept making pecan cheesecake.

Early in 1988, a guest who was getting married asked if we made wedding cakes.

"Yes," I immediately replied. "But we only do chocolate raspberry cakes."

The bride-to-be beamed with excitement at the thought of a chocolate wedding cake. I had never made one, but would give it a try. I cooked on the line all night and at 11 p.m. started making the cake from scratch: the mousse, the glaze, and the ganache. By 3:30 a.m., I was putting the finishing touches on the cake. By the next afternoon the cake had set up well. It looked like a cross between a large chocolate space capsule and the Liberty Bell. I was embarrassed and frustrated. So I went out and got some nice roses, baby breath and some ferns. I gussied up the cake with the flora and garnished it with chocolate truffles. I still was pretty insecure about it and did not know whether the bride would be happy. Well, the bride loved it, and things snowballed. We have been doing chocolate wedding cakes ever since.

Buoyed by the public's love of our desserts and chocolates, Marilyn and I made a brief foray into the bakery business, launching Marifil's at two locations in Traverse City in the mid-1990s. Though highly regarded, Marifil's was a short and sweet experience. I soon returned to my kitchen.

With Windows' increasing success, Marilyn stopped working in 1996 to spend time with our children. Marilyn's guest relations efforts were continued by Mari Chamberlain, who began working with us in 1989. Mari is among Windows' devoted core staff, a loyal and invaluable group of people who have been with the restaurant for years. Some stay for the money; others remain for the intense, high-caliber restaurant atmosphere. Each day at the restaurant begins with The Family Meal, served at 5 p.m. In many ways, Windows employees have become our family.

Our loyal employees have adopted our total dedication to the success of Windows, quickly learning that when they deliver those plates of food, people often are in awe. They absorb that pride. The loyalty often is a two-way street. We have signed car loans for devoted workers and, for employees who strive and who care about what we're doing, we often have cut them slack when needed. Meanwhile, the staff tolerated the years when Marilyn and I, faced with the tension of running the restaurant, were sometimes at each others' throats. They knew our first priority was the restaurant and worked as a team toward high standards.

Some of our staff members met on the job and later married. Chef Randy Chamberlain and cook Corey Luna also have worked with us since the late 1980s. Marilyn has often joked that Windows will one day be the only restaurant with a full staff in wheelchairs.

Mari had been integral in establishing Windows' wine list, a consistent *Spectator* magazine award winner. We felt a high-caliber wine selection was vital to fine dining, and Mari was deft at the game of seeking out and acquiring noted vintages. Once, a group of VIP guests called to schedule a party and I offered them our last case of a hard-to-get California Chardonnay. My manager hurried up to me when he found out.

"Why did you sell them that wine? That's all we had."

"Well," I said, "That's what it's there for."

Windows carries a comprehensive variety of wines from California, France, Italy and around the world, all intended to complement our food selections. We also have one of the most sweeping selections of vintages from northern Michigan's young and growing wine region, located along the 45th parallel on latitudinal par with celebrated French and Italian grape-growing areas. Great Lakes wines, first introduced commercially three decades ago, are gaining prestige. More than a dozen wineries now operate in the area around Windows.

The region's culinary specialties—whitefish, trout, wild leeks, buffalo, cherries and morel mushrooms—also are staples of Windows' menu. During morel season, from April through June, nearly every table orders a plate of the hard-to-find mushrooms, and we incorporate the delicacy into soups and sauces.

By the mid-1990s, Windows was no longer fighting for survival. We were attracting regular clientele, continually upgrading the restaurant's decor, making good money and receiving frequent readers choice awards in local publications such as *Northern Express* and *Traverse: Northern Michigan's Magazine*. I also had the honor of contributing to a cookbook published by Faygo Beverages Inc. in 1997.

In the summer of 1999, my photograph appeared in *Traverse: Northern Michigan's Magazine*. I had tried, in vain, to get a picture of the whole staff, but ended up with a full-page picture of yours truly. I dubbed myself the celebrity chef of the month. It was dart-board size, which came in handy soon after when a nice couple dined at Windows for their anniversary. The gentleman had his heart set on our popular northern star dessert—but we were out. He had dined with us three years before and was similarly disappointed.

Despite such occasional slips, our dedication to high standards and consistent quality have kept guests returning, and they continue to spread the good word about Windows. They return for the lobster, the tournedo Nicholas, and the mixed grill, a feast of quail, duck, lamb, and beef filet. They return for the chocolates, the ice cream, the Mardi Gras revelry, the mix of Creole, northern Michigan, and traditional American cuisine. They return for the view, the joy of fine food, and the pleasures of eating.

I didn't know when I found that five-dollar bill stuck to a plate at Mondo's Restaurant that my dreams of being a chef would lead me to the blue waters of the Great Lakes, where I could view waves every day and feed fine cuisine to northern Michigan residents and visitors. And I didn't know I'd find such joy and satisfaction in preparing food that makes people happy.

Over the years, with my travel through the kitchens of the Midwest, East Coast and New Orleans, I've acquired a number of good recipes, culinary creations that have brought pleasure to my diners. In the pages that follow, many of these recipes appear.

Enjoy, and bon appétit.

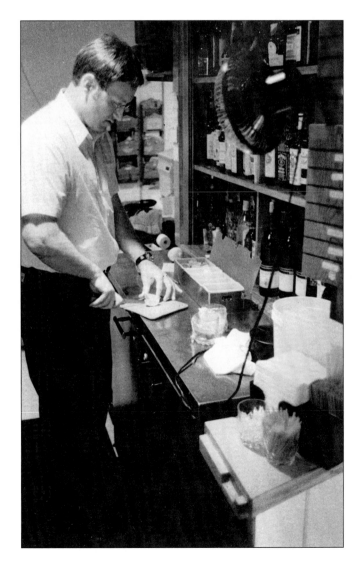

Appetizers and First Courses

MORELS

Fresh morels abound in northern Michigan, usually from late April to early June. Morel hunting is an art form, and thousands descend on the region for annual morel hunts. Some of those fortunate enough to find them call Windows so that they can sell them to us. We are always haggling over the price per pound due to availability.

When we have fresh morels, we put them in any sauce or preparation that requires mushrooms. Our guests are probably surprised to see morels in our beef tenderloin, quail, lamb and veal dishes. Windows also serves the morels à la carte as a special appetizer. When an order of these delicacies leaves our kitchen, the rich, woodsy aroma fills the dining room. Gastronomical noises of pleasure are heard with every bite. This puts other diners in the mood for their own morels.

Before using morels, I soak them in a bowl of medium salted water, adding about a half cup of salt to a gallon of water. Let mushrooms soak for 10 to 12 minutes to give dirt a chance to dislodge and allow any creepy, crawly bugs to come out of hiding. Crunchy beetles and bugs in morel mushrooms do add some good protein, but they are not desirable.

Morel Mushrooms with Vidalia Onions and Asparagus

SERVES FOUR

This exquisite appetizer is new at Windows. We wanted to try a morel dish that had fewer calories and tasted good. With morels, asparagus and Vidalia onions all in season simultaneously, it had to turn out to be a good combination.

1 medium Vidalia onion, cut julienne style

8 ounces fresh morel mushrooms

8 to 12 fresh asparagus tips, pre-poached

2 tablespoons unsalted butter

1 cup chicken broth or veal stock

1 jigger of excellent brandy or sherry

White pepper and salt to taste

Heat 8- to 10-inch sauté pan until hot and add 1 tablespoon of butter. Add cut onions, cooking until lightly caramelized. Cooking the onions first helps extract natural sugars, making a sweeter end product. After onions cook, add morels. Sauté for 1 minute, then add brandy or sherry and flame off alcohol. Add stock and simmer for 10 to 12 minutes. Remove from heat. Stir in remaining butter and add pre-poached asparagus tips. Season with salt and white pepper. Pour in serving dish and garnish the top with asparagus spears.

Morel Mushroom Appetizer

Morel Mushrooms
Stewed in Brandy Creme

SERVES FOUR

2 teaspoons unsalted butter

2 cups morel mushrooms

$^1/_2$ teaspoon shallots

2 ounces brandy

$^1/_2$ cup whole cream

$^1/_2$ cup beef stock or bouillon

White pepper and salt

Use a 10-inch sauté pan. Get pan hot and add butter. Sizzle, add shallots, then mushrooms. Sauté for 1 minute. Add brandy away from heat, and then put pan back on heat to flame out alcohol. Add whole cream. Simmer until thick and bubbly. Add beef stock or bouillon. Simmer 5 to 6 minutes or until thick and creamy. Season with dash of salt and white pepper. This appetizer can be eaten by itself or used for dipping with French bread. This wonderful concoction may also be used on steaks, chicken, veal or pork.

Portobello Mushroom Appetizer

SERVES FOUR

Fresh, large portobellos have a steak-like quality and are very healthy, especially simmered in lots of garlic, shallots and wine.

4 large portobello mushrooms, cleaned and de-stemmed

2 tablespoons olive oil

3 tablespoons chopped garlic

6 ounces chicken or beef stock

6 ounces sherry or port wine

White pepper and salt to taste

Add olive oil to a 10- to 12-inch sauté pan or 3-quart sauce pot. Add garlic and shallots. Sauté for 30-45 seconds. Add mushrooms and wine. Simmer until wine has been reduced by half. Add stock and simmer for 10 to 12 minutes or until mushrooms become very tender. When mushrooms are cooked, take out of pan. Slice julienne or in triangles. Season sauce with pepper and salt. Pour sauce on platter and serve mushrooms on top.

Paneed Chevre with Tomato Rosemary Cream, Pistachios and Sun-Dried Tomato Garlic Compote

SERVES FOUR TO SIX

8-ounce log of chevre cheese

3 ounces clarified butter

$^1/_2$ tablespoon whole, unsalted butter

$^1/_2$ teaspoon minced garlic

$^1/_4$ teaspoon minced shallot

2 ounces sun-dried tomatoes, sliced julienne style

2 ounces toasted pistachios

2 eggs and 1 ounce water beaten together (egg wash)

$^1/_2$ cup all-purpose flour

2 cups roasted French bread crumbs

2 to 3 fresh rosemary sprigs

6 to 8 ounces tomato rosemary cream (see recipe below)

Use a heated French knife to cut chevre into $^1/_2$-inch round slices. Flour chevre and dip in egg wash. Place chevre in bread crumbs and set aside. Place clarified butter in a 10- to 12-inch sauté pan and get hot. Sauté breaded chevre slices until golden brown on both sides. Set chevre aside. Dump out excess fat. Place $^1/_2$ tablespoon of whole butter in sauté pan. Get hot and sizzle minced garlic and shallots. Add sun-dried tomatoes. Season with salt and pepper and set aside. Place tomato rosemary sauce on a warm plate. Place warm chevre on top of sauce. Place sun-dried tomato compote in center. Garnish with toasted pistachios and fresh rosemary.

Rosemary Cream

SERVES FOUR TO SIX

6 sprigs fresh rosemary

8 ounces white wine

1 teaspoon shallots, minced

10 ounces heavy cream

2 tablespoons fine Italian tomato paste

White pepper and salt to taste

Place shallots, rosemary and white wine in sauce pot. Simmer until reduced by half. Add whole cream, simmer 20 minutes, then stir in tomato paste. Simmer 2 to 4 more minutes. Strain and season with white pepper and salt.

Chevre appetizer

Seared Sea Scallops with Garlic Sauce

SERVES FOUR

Sea scallops are one of the most delicious of the ocean's seafood. It is imperative that they be very fresh. They should be firm and sweet smelling. The first challenge is finding a fresh scallop. The fish markets in Venice have them. We try to obtain dry-pack scallops, which are the freshest and packed naturally.

8 to 12 large fresh sea scallops

$^1/_8$ teaspoon oil (soybean or canola)

$^1/_2$ teaspoon chopped shallots

2 teaspoons chopped garlic

1 cup white wine

1 tablespoon soft unsalted butter

Juice of $^1/_2$ lemon

Fresh parsley

White pepper and salt to taste

Preheat oven to 400 degrees.

Get a sauté pan very hot and add oil. Add sea scallops, sear until golden brown on both sides. Place pan with scallops in oven for 8 to 10 minutes. In the meantime, put shallots, garlic and white wine in a sauté pan. Cook until wine is reduced by half. Take wine, garlic and shallot mixture off the heat. Stir in whole butter. Add lemon juice. Salt and pepper to taste. Pour mixture onto a plate, add sea scallops and garnish with fresh chopped parsley and lemon.

Mussels Provencal

SERVES FOUR FOR DINNER OR EIGHT AS AN APPETIZER

48 to 50 fresh mussels

2 tablespoons olive oil

$^1/_4$ cup chopped garlic

$^1/_8$ cup shallots

2 tablespoons capers

2 large fresh tomatoes, medium diced

2 cups white wine

2 tablespoons fresh chopped parsley

Juice of 2 lemons

White pepper and salt to taste

Get olive oil hot in a 12- to 14-inch sauté pan. Add garlic, shallots, mussels, tomatoes, capers and white wine. Bring to a boil. Cover pan and simmer for 6 to 8 minutes. Season with lemon juice, salt and pepper. Garnish with fresh chopped parsley.

Windows' Smoked Whitefish Pâté

SERVES FOUR TO SIX

Windows gets its smoked whitefish from Carlson's Fishery in Leland. Their technique and style of smoking whitefish is fantastic. It comes with the skin on and the bones in, which we remove. The remaining smoked fish is very moist, succulent and tasty. This appetizer has been one of our most popular over the years.

1 pound smoked whitefish filet meat, cleaned and deboned

1³/₄ pounds cream cheese

Worcestershire sauce to taste

Tabasco sauce to taste

Place cleaned smoked whitefish in electric mixing bowl and mix on slow speed for 1 minute. Stop mixer. Look inside bowl for any bones that may have been missed. They will stick out like a sore thumb. Add cream cheese and mix for 2 minutes on medium speed. Scrape mixing bowl. Mix again for 1 minute. Make sure that all smoked whitefish and cream cheese is mixed well. Season very lightly with Tabasco and Worcestershire sauces. Serve with crackers and jalapeño salsa (see recipe below). Also can be served hot, baked in a casserole.

Jalapeño Salsa

MAKES ABOUT SIX CUPS

1 medium Spanish onion

1 medium Bermuda onion

3 peppers, one each of red, yellow and green

3 cups fresh tomatoes

1 tablespoon jalapeño pepper

2 tablespoons chopped parsley

1 tablespoon cracked black pepper

1 teaspoon salt

¹/₃ cup balsamic vinegar

2 tablespoons olive oil

Juice of one lemon

Finely dice all vegetables. Mix all ingredients. Best when marinated for a few days. Serve with smoked whitefish pâté. This recipe is pretty simple.

Bisques, Soups and Stews

Butternut Squash Bisque

2¹/₂ pounds peeled, diced butternut squash

2 ounces chopped shallots

8 chopped baker potatoes, peeled and rough cut

3 large Spanish onions, peeled and rough cut with root removed

4 cups chicken stock

4 cups whole cream

2 cups milk

¹/₂ cup whole butter

2 tablespoons vegetable oil

¹/₂ teaspoon ground allspice

¹/₄ teaspoon ground nutmeg

4 to 6 bay leaves

White pepper and salt to taste

Place butter and oil in soup pot. Get hot. Add onions, and slowly caramelize, then add shallots, potatoes, butternut squash, allspice and nutmeg. Simmer 8 to 10 minutes. Add stock, cream, milk and bay leaves. Bring to a slow boil. Simmer for 30 to 40 minutes or until potatoes are tender. Fish out bay leaves and purée soup. Season with salt and white pepper.

Smoked Whitefish Chowder

Smoked Whitefish Stock

1 whole smoked whitefish (approximately 2lbs.)

4-6 bay leaves

1 teaspoon thyme leaves

1 teaspoon oregano leaves

2 carrots rough chopped

1 medium Spanish onion rough chopped with skin

2-3 celery stalks rough chopped

2 quarts water

Remove all smoked whitefish meat and dice small, set aside. Save bones for stock.

In a 4-6 quart sauce pot, place smoked whitefish bones, bay leaves, thyme, oregano, onion, carrots, celery, and water, and bring to a slow boil, and simmer for approximately two hours. When stock is finished strain through a large holed china cap and set aside.

Chowder

2 medium Spanish onions

1 bunch of medium celery

2 leeks

1 medium sweet red pepper

1 medium sweet yellow pepper

5 peeled russet baker potatoes (peel, dice into 1/2-inch segments and store in water until ready for use)

6 shucked ears of corn, and shave off kernels

1 tablespoon chopped garlic

Clean and dice all vegetables in 1/4 to 1/2-inch dice

8 ounces of unsalted butter

8 ounces of all purpose flour

1 quart milk or whole cream

Place butter in 4-6 quart soup pot. Let butter start to sizzle. Add all vegetables except potatoes. Simmer for 5 minutes. Add flour, stir on low heat for 10-12 minutes. This is cooking the roux, for the soup. After cooking this add smoked whitefish stock; bring to a slow boil. As soon as it just starts to boil, add diced potatoes, simmer 30 minutes. While soup is simmering, in a separate pot heat up milk or cream.

As soon as milk becomes scalding add to soup. Simmer 10 more minutes; add diced smoked whitefish meat. Season with Tabasco sauce and a little white pepper. Do not season with salt, because smoked whitefish has plenty of salt already.

Serve with fresh crusty French bread.

Bouillabaisse

SERVES FOUR TO SIX

Two 1¹/₂-pound live Maine lobsters

12 jumbo shrimp

8 large sea scallops

24 fresh mussels

8 cherry stone clams

*2 pounds assorted fish filet—tuna, salmon, mahi mahi,
monkfish, sole, etc.—cut in 2-inch chunks*

6 stone crab claws, cracked

3 carrots, rough chopped

1 bunch celery, rough chopped

2 large Spanish onions, rough chopped

3 to 4 shallots, rough chopped

*Bouquet garni: a few parsley sprigs, some fresh thyme,
oregano and rosemary tied in a bunch*

6 bay leaves

4 whole bulbs of garlic, cut in half

6 tablespoons chopped garlic

4 tablespoons olive oil

2 teaspoons saffron

2 cups of fine Italian tomato paste

2 tablespoons Brandy

Juice of two lemons

2 quarts water or fish stock

White pepper and salt to taste

Split the lobster heads in half with a French knife. Set lobster heads aside. Twist off claws and tails, then blanch in boiling water for 2 minutes. Cool and set aside. Steam cherry stone clams ahead and let cool. Peel shrimp and save shells. Dice fish filets into chunks and save scraps. Take shrimp, scallops, fish chunks and mix with 2 tablespoons of olive oil, 2 tablespoons chopped garlic, season with salt and white pepper. Let marinate and set aside.

In a large soup pot, place 2 tablespoons of olive oil and get smoking hot. Add lobster heads and sear until nice and red. Add shrimp shells, fish scraps, rough chopped vegetables, whole garlic bulbs cut in half. Let ingredients get hot. Stir often. Add brandy, flame. Add tomato paste, saffron and bouquet garni. Add water or stock, bring to a slow boil. Let simmer on low for 2 hours. When stock is done cooking, strain through a large whole china cap or colander.

In a cleaned soup pot, add olive oil, get hot. Add shrimp, fish chunks, scallops and mussels, and sauté. Add 2 tablespoons of chopped garlic. Add brandy, and flame. Add stock. Bring to a low boil. Simmer for 6 to 8 minutes. When fish and shellfish are cooked, add pre-steamed clams, blanched lobster and stone crabs, and simmer for 2 minutes. Add the juice of two lemons. Season with white pepper and salt. Serve.

In preparing a delicious and tasty bouillabaisse, it is very important that you use the freshest seafood. It will take just one small bad or old piece of seafood to ruin the whole batch. When you strain the stock make sure that you use a large holed china cap and/or colander. This will allow some of the fish and shellfish pieces to strain through to your final product. Also, during the cooking process, by letting the seafood stock come to a simmer through a low heat process you will get a more rich tasting and delicious product.

Bouillabaisse

Carrot Ginger Bisque

MAKES ABOUT 1 GALLON

3 ounces of unsalted butter

15-20 medium sized sweet carrots peeled and rough chopped (Try tasting carrots for sweetness)

2 medium Spanish onions, peeled medium diced with root cut out

6 russet baker potatoes peeled, diced $\frac{1}{2}$ inch

2 teaspoons diced shallots

4-5 tablespoons finely diced fresh ginger

1 quart of chicken stock or water

1 quart of milk or whole cream

4-6 bay leaves

Salt, white pepper and Tabasco

In a 4-6 quart stock pot, add 3 ounces of unsalted butter, sizzle, add chopped onions, slow cook for 10-12 minutes, or until onions become translucent, add diced shallots, ginger, diced potatoes and carrots, let steep 10 minutes on low heat.

Add water or chicken stock, add bay leaves. Bring to a slow simmer. Let cook 20-25 minutes or until potatoes and carrots become nice and tender.

In a separate pot scald cream or milk, add to soup, simmer 5 minutes. To finish soup, fish out bay leaves with a slotted spoon. Purée remaining ingredients until smooth and creamy. Season to taste with salt, white pepper and Tabasco.

This soup can be served well in puff pastry domes. Pour soup in an ovenproof bowl, leaving a $\frac{1}{2}$-inch gap in bowl and let cool. Cut out puff pastry in shape of bowl. Eggwash rim of bowl. Place puff pastry on top of bowl. Lightly eggwash top puff pastry. Bake for 20 minutes at 400 degrees or until crispy and brown. Serve hot and the aroma of ginger and sweet carrots will permeate as soon as you break into the puff pastry crust.

Roasted Garlic Bisque

MAKES ABOUT ONE GALLON

1¹/₂ pounds peeled garlic cloves

6 ounces chopped shallots

6 baker potatoes, peeled and rough chopped

3 large Spanish onions, peeled and rough cut with root removed

4 cups chicken stock

4 cups whole cream

2 cups milk

¹/₂ cup olive oil

4 to 6 bay leaves

White pepper and salt to taste

Season garlic cloves with $1/4$ cup olive oil, salt and white pepper. Roast in oven at 325 degrees for 30 to 40 minutes or until golden brown. While garlic is in oven, place remaining olive oil in soup pot and get hot. Add onions and caramelize for 6 to 8 minutes. Add shallots and potatoes. Continue to cook on low heat until roasted garlic is ready. Add roasted garlic, bay leaves, chicken stock, whole cream and milk. Bring to a slow boil. Simmer 30 to 40 minutes. When potatoes are soft, soup is finished cooking. Fish out bay leaves. Puree soup and season with salt and white pepper.

Entrées

Whitefish Pecandine

SERVES FOUR

This preparation is one of Windows' signature dishes. It has been on our menu since the late 1980s, and whenever I bring a dish for the Leland Wine Festival, this is what I serve.

I purchase fresh Lake Superior whitefish from William King & Sons Fisheries. I do this to emphasize the freshness. When we receive our fish it is out of the water for barely twelve hours. To prepare the whitefish for cooking, we receive it partially filleted, but more remains to be done and this is where the fun begins. First we pull out all the pin bones from the center of the filets using needle-nose pliers. Once done, we cut off excess fat. Then, with a long slicing knife, the skin is removed. Now the whitefish is ready to be cooked.

*4 whitefish filets,
pin-boned and skinned*

*4 eggs and 2 tablespoons water,
mixed together*

2 cups flour

2 teaspoons Creole seasoning

4 cups dried, roasted French bread crumbs

12 ounces clarified butter or canola oil

1 cup toasted pecans

Juice of 2 lemons

1 tablespoon whole unsalted butter

Preheat oven to 400 degrees.

Season filets liberally with Creole seasoning, dredge in flour and shake off excess. Dip completely in egg wash, place in French bread crumbs and pat dry. Use a 12- to 14-inch skillet or sauté pan. Add oil and get it very hot (if it's not hot, fish will be soggy). Add whitefish filets. They will start to fry immediately. Once the outside is crispy, flip over with a spatula. Cook for 2-3 minutes.

Place whitefish filet on platter. Empty sauté pan. Add whole unsalted butter. Sizzle and add pecans. Sauté 15 seconds. Squeeze lemon over pecans, pour over fish.

Fresh Walleye
Paneed with Shrimp in a Sun-Dried Tomato Garlic Cream Sauce

SERVES FOUR

4 walleye filets,
boned and skinned

1 tablespoon Creole seasoning

1 cup all-purpose flour

3 eggs

2 cups dry roasted bread crumbs

8 ounces clarified butter mixed with
2 ounces vegetable oil

Season walleye filet liberally with Creole seasoning. Dredge in flour and shake off excess. Dip in beaten egg. Dip filets in bread crumbs (make sure they are fully coated with bread crumbs). In a 12- to 14-inch sauté pan, get clarified butter and oil mixture very hot—at least to 350 degrees or to point where bread crumb dropped in oil will sizzle. Pan fry walleye until crispy on one side. Flip over with a spatula. Place the whole pan of fish in a 350-degree oven for 5 to 6 minutes. While fish is in oven, start making the sauce.

Shrimp in Sun-Dried Tomato Garlic Cream Sauce

MAKES SAUCE FOR FOUR WALLEYE

1 tablespoon whole unsalted butter

12 jumbo shrimp, peeled and deveined

2 tablespoons chopped garlic

1 teaspoon chopped shallot

2 tablespoons poached julienne sun-dried tomatoes

2 cups whole cream

2 tablespoons grated Parmesan cheese

White pepper and salt to taste

In a 10-inch sauté pan or 2-quart sauce pot, melt butter and sauté shallots and garlic for 30 to 45 seconds. Add shrimp, sun-dried tomato strips and whole cream. Bring to a boil, simmer 8 to 10 minutes or until shrimp are fully cooked. Add Parmesan cheese. Season to taste. Place cooked walleye filet on a plate or platter and garnish each filet with shrimp. Spoon sauce on top. Serve.

Paneed Walleye

Norwegian Salmon
Oven Roasted with Capers and Lemon Butter

SERVES SIX TO EIGHT

This fish is one of the most popular and versatile fish of the sea. Our salmon repertoire includes char-grilled with artichokes and mushrooms, pan sautéed Florentine, en croute (baked in puff pastry and filled with a jardiniere of vegetables), poached in court bouillon, steamed with lemon butter, smoked, gravlaxed and numerous other presentations. Our most popular salmon is slowly oven roasted with capers and lemon, ingredients that complement salmon's flavor.

When looking for salmon, make sure it has firm, sweet-smelling flesh and clear eyes. Cut away bones and clear away the full two sides of the salmon. At Windows, we also cut off the belly section. Next, we take a pair of needle-nosed pliers and pull out all the pin bones. We cut off the skin with a long sharp slicer knife. Once the skin is off and all the bones have been removed, turn the filet over and trim away all the gray area, which is fat. An average-size salmon is about 7 to 9 pounds. When you finish cleaning the salmon you should get at least three to four portions out of each filet, enough to feed six to eight guests.

Six to eight 6-to 7-ounce salmon filets

8 ounces of capers drained

1 ounce finely diced shallots

3 cups lemon butter (See recipe for Paupiettes of Lemon Sole)

2 lemons

White pepper and salt

Spread finely diced shallots on a 12-inch baking pan. Place salmon filets on top. Season lightly with salt and white pepper. Lightly coat salmon with lemon butter. Liberally garnish top of filets with capers. Bake in a 325-degree oven for about 15 to 20 minutes. Garnish with lemon wedges and serve.

Norwegian Salmon

Mahi Mahi
With Grilled Shrimp and Shiitake Mushrooms

SERVES SIX TO EIGHT

Mahi mahi is a wonderful, sweet-tasting saltwater fish, abundant from the Gulf of Mexico to the shores of Hawaii. Mahi is considered an excellent sport fish and a delicacy to eat. One of the most interesting mahi mahi recipes I have run across comes from my lifelong friend Wilber (alias Ron). He lives in Florida and fishes a great deal. Wilber suggested taking 3-ounce mahi filets, making a batter by adding beer to Aunt Jemima pancake mix, dipping the mahi mahi in the batter and cooking it like pancakes. At first I thought this was a real goofy idea. My curiosity got the best of me and I tried it. It's delicious.

Mahi mahi arrives at the restaurant with the skin on, and it requires lots of work to prepare it properly. First, we cut off the belly and excess fat. Then we cut off the skin. The remaining filet has a row of bones and fat in the middle. We then cut through the filet's middle and cut out the bony section, which leaves two pieces. We then turn the filet over and trim all of the dark fatty tissue away. This is where a lot of the fishy taste comes from improperly cleaned fish. After the mahi mahi is cleaned and completely trimmed of all excess fat and sinews, we wash it in icy cold water. We then cut the large filets to resemble small filets, two to four ounces each, so we can quickly pan fry or sauté the mahi mahi.

18 pieces of 2-to 3-ounce mahi mahi medallions, cleaned and trimmed

36 jumbo white raw shrimp, peeled, deveined and lightly seasoned with vegetable oil, salt and white pepper

8 to 10 medium shiitake mushrooms, cleaned and cut julienne style

12 ounces clarified butter

4 ounces whole unsalted butter

2 ounces Creole seasoning

3 lemons

2 cups all-purpose flour

3 eggs beaten with 1 tablespoon water

Season mahi mahi filets with Creole seasoning. Dredge in flour and let soak in beaten egg mixture. Place clarified butter in a 12- to 14-inch sauté pan. Once pan is hot, take out filets, run thumb and index finger down filets to remove excess egg wash, and sauté for 2 minutes on each side until a light golden brown. When mahi mahi goes into pan, place shrimp on grill and cook 2 minutes on each side. When fish is finished, empty out sauté pan and place mahi mahi in a warm place. Add whole butter to the sauté pan, then add shiitake mushrooms. Sauté until soft, about 1 minute. Squeeze the juice of 2 lemons into mushrooms. Season with salt and white pepper. Place mushrooms on platter. Place warm mahi mahi on top of mushrooms. Garnish with the grilled shrimp. Squeeze the remaining lemon's juice over shrimp and serve.

Paupiettes of Lemon Sole Florentine

SERVES FOUR

Eight 6- to 8-ounce filets of lemon sole

1 teaspoon diced shallots

16 ounces fresh baby spinach

8 to 10 ounces lemon butter (see recipe below)

2 tablespoons whole butter

White pepper and salt to taste

Filet of sole should be sweet smelling and firm. Cut the center of the filet out, which is the section that has the bones. After cutting out the bone section, 16 half filets should remain. Turn filets so dark side is up. Trim any excess fat or non-white portions on the filets. Lightly season with white pepper and salt. Roll filets up like a jelly roll. Lightly coat a cookie sheet with 1 tablespoon of whole butter. Sprinkle chopped shallots. Place rolled lemon sole filets on cookie sheet. Gently nap or cover filets with lemon butter. Bake in a 325-degree oven for about 15 to 20 minutes. About 5 minutes before sole is done, place a 12- to 14-inch sauté pan on stove with 1 tablespoon of whole butter and sauté the baby spinach. Season with white pepper and salt. Place cooked spinach on a warm platter. When sole is done, place it on top of spinach and serve.

Lemon Butter

MAKES 12 OUNCES

1 teaspoon diced shallots

8 ounces whole butter, cubed

1 cup white wine

Juice of one lemon

2 ounces whole cream

In a 2-quart sauce pot, place shallots and white wine. Reduce by half. Add whole cream and simmer 5 to 6 minutes. Slowly whip in whole butter on a very low heat. Butter will incorporate like a warm mayonnaise. When butter is incorporated, take off heat and season with white pepper, salt and lemon juice. Use this sauce for coating the sole. Or it can be used as a dipping sauce for lobster and shrimp.

Yellow Fin Tuna Tamari
Char-grilled with Jumbo Shrimp, Garnished with Whole-Grain Mustard Butter

SERVES FOUR

Four 8-ounce fresh center-cut tuna filets, trimmed of skin and dark fatty tissues, leaving a deep red, fresh, sweet-smelling filet

12 jumbo shrimp, peeled and deveined

4 ounces tamari, mixed with 2 ounces water

8 ounces lemon butter (See recipe for Paupiettes of Lemon Sole)

5 ounces excellent French whole-grain mustard

2 ounces fresh chopped parsley

4 fresh rosemary sprigs

After tuna filets have been completely trimmed, place filets and jumbo shrimp in tamari and water marinade. Let marinade about 30 minutes. Get grill nice and hot. Place tuna on grill along with shrimp. Fully cook shrimp. Cook tuna to desired temperature.

Mix whole-grain mustard with warm lemon butter and pour on serving platter. Place tuna and shrimp on top of sauce. Garnish with fresh rosemary and chopped parsley, then serve.

Lobster Vivant

SERVES FOUR

Four 1¹/₂-pound live Maine lobsters

16 medium-sized shrimp,
peeled and deveined

4 tablespoons whole unsalted butter

1 teaspoon diced shallots

1 ounce brandy

4 cups sea scallops or rock shrimp

1 cup white wine

¹/₄ cup Dijon mustard

¹/₂ cup dry roasted French bread crumbs

2 cups lemon butter

White pepper and salt to taste

Take a 3-gallon stock pot and fill it ³/₄ full of water. Bring to a roiling boil. Blanch lobsters for 6 minutes. Take out of water; let cool. Once lobster is cool, gently twist off claws and knuckles. Split bodies in half lengthwise and remove coral and tail meat. Set aside. Wash out body cavity and set aside. To remove claw meat, pull out bottom claw piece first. Detach knuckles. With a French knife, crack the bottom portion of the main claw. Twist knife in the crack of the claw to remove an end piece of the claw. The claw meat will come out in one whole piece; set aside. Crack remaining knuckles in half with a French knife and remove meat; set aside.

In a 10-inch sauté pan, add 1 tablespoon of butter. Sizzle shallots. Add shrimp and season with white pepper and salt. Let sauté for 1 minute. Cook shrimp half way. Flame with brandy and let cool. In a 10-inch sauté pan, add butter, sizzle, then add sea scallops or rock shrimp. Sauté 1 minute, then add white wine and cook for 1 minute. Add mustard and lobster knuckle meat. Stir in French bread crumbs and let cool.

Place partially cooked shrimp inside tail sections. Place scallop mixture into body cavity. Lightly coat with lemon butter and bake in a 350-degree oven for 12 to 14 minutes. During the last 3 minutes, lightly coat lobster tail meat and claws with lemon butter and bake for 2 minutes. When nice and hot, place tail meat and claws on top of lobster bodies and serve.

Lobster Vivant

Crab Cake or Crab Puffs

MAKES EIGHT 6-OUNCE CRAB CAKES OR SIXTEEN 3-OUNCE CRAB PUFFS

This crab mix recipe can be served cold as a salad accompaniment, as a garnish on a canape or baked in a casserole garnished with bread crumbs and Hungarian paprika. This is tender, sweet blue lump crab, tossed in a house-made dressing of mayonnaise, whole-grain mustard, capers, lemon juice, Tabasco sauce and a touch of Creole seasoning and dry roasted bread crumbs. Crab cakes are formed with a 4-ounce scoop and shaped like a flying saucer, whereas the crab puff is round.

2 pounds jumbo lump crab meat from the blue crab

2 pounds lump crab meat from the blue crab

3 eggs

3 cups vegetable oil

4 ounces clarified butter mixed together with
4 ounces salad oil to sauté crab cakes

$^1/_4$ cup French whole-grain mustard

$^1/_2$ cup capers

2 teaspoons Worcestershire sauce

Juice of 2 lemons

3-5 drops Tabasco sauce

2$^1/_2$ cups dry roasted French bread crumbs

White pepper and salt to taste

Creole seasoning to taste

Clean crab meat by taking out cartilage and shell pieces, taking care to leave in orange pieces, which are crab fat. Do this very carefully, keeping crab in the largest possible pieces. Set crab meat aside in refrigerator. In a mixing bowl, whip 3 whole eggs at high speed. Slowly incorporate the 3 cups of vegetable oil to make the mayonnaise. Then add mustard, capers, Worcestershire, lemon juice and Tabasco. Mix well. Taste mix. Season with white pepper and salt to taste. Gently fold crab meat into mixture. Fold in one cup of bread crumbs. The crab mix should start to hold together. Add more bread crumbs if needed. Scoop crab mix into 6-ounce patties. Roll crab cake in remaining bread crumbs. Gently pack crab cake like a thick flying saucer.

In a 12-inch sauté pan, add clarified butter and salad oil mix. Get hot. Sauté crab cakes until crispy on one side. Flip over with spatula. Place in a 350-degree oven for 3 to 4 minutes. Serve.

For crab puffs, scoop 3-ounce puffs into round balls. Roll in bread crumb pack like a loose snowball. Sauté until crispy golden brown all over.

Soft-Shell Crabs Pecandine

SERVES FOUR TO SIX

Every year about the second week of May we get calls asking whether our soft-shell crabs have arrived yet. We then call Shore Seafood in Saxis, Virginia. If the weather has been good, they ship us live soft-shell crabs. We usually order the whale size, the largest that they harvest. The crabs are packed in straw within a cardboard container and flown in an air-tight container via Federal Express. Shipping costs more than the actual crabs. When they arrive, we open the box to make sure that they are fresh, then call our anxious soft-shell crab lovers to tell them they're in.

Cleaning fresh soft-shell crabs can be a little squeamish. We cut out the eyes, the digestive tracts or aprons, and the lungs beneath the flaps. Then they're ready to be cooked.

6 large fresh soft-shell crabs, cleaned

2 cups all-purpose flour

2-3 teaspoons Creole seasoning

$1/2$ cup clarified butter

1 cup roasted unsalted pecan pieces

2 lemons

2 tablespoons whole unsalted butter

After crabs have been cleaned, season the undersides with Creole seasoning. Take a large 14- to 16-inch skillet or sauté pan and add clarified butter. Get hot. Dredge crabs in flour. Shake off excess flour, and sauté crabs in hot clarified butter until crispy, about 3 to 5 minutes per side. Place crabs on serving platter. Dump excess fat from pan. Add whole butter to hot sauté pan. Sizzle butter, toss in pecan pieces, cut lemons in half, squeeze lemon juice into pecans, and pour over sautéed soft shells.

Barbecued Shrimp

SERVES FOUR TO SIX

Barbecued shrimp is a very spicy, very popular entree and appetizer at Windows. This rendition results from quite a few years of experimentation. It is quite delicious.

24 to 30 jumbo shrimp, peeled and deveined

2 tablespoons whole butter

4 tablespoons chopped garlic

2 tablespoons chopped shallots

2 tablespoons cracked black pepper

4 tablespoons Creole seasoning

3 to 4 fresh rosemary sprigs

One 12-ounce lager beer or shrimp stock

Juice from 2 lemons

Dash of salt

Get a 12- to 14-inch sauté pan hot on stove. Add butter, sizzle and add garlic and shallots. Cook for 30 seconds. Add shrimp. Sauté while adding cracked pepper, Creole seasoning, rosemary and lager beer or shrimp stock. Bring to a boil. Simmer 5 to 6 minutes or until shrimp is done. Season with fresh-squeezed lemon and a dash of salt. Serve in a bowl with crusty French bread for sopping up the sauce.

Duck Confit
With Lyonnaise Potatoes and a Shiitake Mushroom Bordelaise

SERVES FOUR TO SIX

Two whole dressed 4- to 5-pound ducks

2 tablespoons water

3 tablespoons cracked black pepper

1 cup whole bay leaves

3 tablespoons sea salt

1 large Spanish onion, cut julienne style

*1 pound sliced blanched redskins or
Yukon gold potatoes*

1 teaspoon Hungarian paprika

1 rough-cut carrot

1 chopped onion

1 stalk celery

Bouquet garni

White pepper and salt to taste

Fresh rosemary sprigs

Take the two ducks and trim all loose skin and fat and place in a 2-quart sauce pot with 2 tablespoons water. Split ducks down the center of the sternum with a French knife. Use French knife to cut out the back section. Save bones and roast them off with the rough-cut vegetables and bouquet garni to make 1 quart of duck stock. Once ducks are cut in half, cut again between the thigh and the beginning of the breast. You will have eight pieces of duck. Trim only excess fat and skin and place in pot with other skin, fat and water. Place pot with fat, skin and water and start to render on the stove. Cook on medium heat for about 30 to 45 minutes to render fat and until remaining skin is crispy. (Crispy duck skin makes an excellent snack mixed with Tabasco sauce.) Strain fats and set aside.

Season duck pieces with the 2 tablespoons cracked pepper, 2 tablespoons sea salt and bay leaves. It is best to let duck pieces marinate overnight.

To cook off ducks, melt duck fat in an 8-quart casserole dish or pot that has a lid. Place duck pieces in covered pot. Braise in oven for $2^{1}/_{2}$ to 3 hours at 300°, or until duck is tender and the remaining bones easily come off duck.

Take duck out of fat and let cool. Once cool, remove rib bones and any excess cartilage. Leave in the large wing bone on the breast (trim down the size of the bone). Also leave in the leg and thigh bone. This technique will help keep duck meat together and have a better-looking presentation. Place the duck inside a casserole dish and pour over the remaining warm duck fat. This technique will allow you to marinate and preserve the duck for a later date.

To serve the duck, get a 12- to 14-inch sauté pan very hot. Take duck out of fat and place skin-side down in sauté pan and roast in a 400-degree oven until duck is crispy on the outside and moist and succulent inside, about 12-15 minutes.

While the duck is in the oven, use a 10-inch sauté pan to make Lyonnaise potatoes. Place 2 tablespoons of duck fat in pan. Add onions and caramelize. Add sliced blanched potatoes, season with 1 tablespoon cracked pepper, 1 tablespoon sea salt and paprika. Mix well and finish baking in oven.

To serve, place Lyonnaise potatoes on a platter, put crispy duck on top. Garnish with sauce (see recipe page 100) around the platter and fresh rosemary sprigs. Enjoy.

Duck Confit Sauce

SERVES FOUR TO SIX

1 tablespoon duck fat

1 teaspoon diced shallot

8 ounces sliced shiitake mushrooms

2 ounces brandy or sherry

4 cups duck stock

White pepper and salt to taste

Take 1 tablespoon duck fat and get it hot in a 1-quart sauce pot. Sizzle shallots, add shiitake mushrooms, flame off brandy, add 4 cups duck stock. Bring to a boil. Simmer 30 minutes or until reduced by half. Season with white pepper and salt to taste.

Helpful Hints on Duck Confit

This Duck confit recipe is great for serving on holidays. It makes a real treat to serve on Christmas Eve. One important warning: when you place the cooked duck skin side down in the hot sauté pan and then place it in a 400 degree oven; when it is coated with fat make sure that there are no loose rivets in the pan handle. You most definitely do not want duck fat dripping out of the pan and into the bottom of the oven and smoking the whole inside of your house so that you cannot see or breathe. Which in turn on Christmas Eve you do not want fire trucks, ambulances and the fire chief coming to your house and double-checking on you! Luckily we had some chocolate oranges to give to the firemen.

Duck Confit

Breast of Chicken Ala May

SERVES FOUR

This dish is dedicated to May and Doc Ruhmann, regular customers at the restaurant for many years who dine with us at least twice a week. May only orders our chicken Boursin, crispy on both sides and cooked well done. After ordering the same chicken dish for five years, we finally named it in May's honor. To May, this was the equivalent of having a road or hospital wing named after her. She was ecstatic!

4 boneless skinless organic Amish chicken breasts

1 ounce vegetable oil

1 cup all-purpose flour

1/2 teaspoon shallots

1/4 cup white wine

2 tablespoons whole cream

6 ounces Leelanau garlic cheese or French Boursin cheese

1 ounce fresh chives

White pepper and salt to taste

In a 12- to 14-inch sauté pan, add vegetable oil and heat. Season chicken breasts with white pepper and salt. Dredge in flour, shake off excess. Sauté breasts until they are really crispy on both sides.

Remove breasts from pan. Finish cooking breasts in a 350-degree oven for 6 to 8 minutes. Pour out excess fat from sauté pan. Deglaze pan with white wine and shallots. Add whole cream and stir with spoon. When liquid is reduced by half turn off heat. Stir in cheese until it is melted. Pour cheese mixture onto platter, place crispy chicken breasts on top. Garnish with fresh chopped chives.

Chubby Chicken

SERVES FOUR TO SIX

Two 6-to 8-ounce chicken breasts, halved

4 ounces crab meat

1 lobster tail, partially blanched

1/2 teaspoon minced shallots

1/2 ounce brandy

1 ounce butter

Puff pastry dough

White pepper and salt to taste

Preheat oven to 350 degrees.

Salt and pepper chicken breast halves. Lightly sauté crab and lobster meat in butter, salt and pepper. Flame with brandy. Put sautéed crab and lobster meat on top of chicken breast halves. Encase each half in puff pastry dough. Coat pastry with beaten raw egg. Bake in oven for 30 to 35 minutes.

Chubby Chicken Sauce

MAKES 1/2 CUP

1 teaspoon shallots

1/2 cup white wine

1/4 cup whole cream

1/2 pound butter

Bring shallots and white wine to a boil in small pan. Reduce by half. Add whole cream and reduce by half again. Lower heat and simmer. Slowly beat in butter, making sure it doesn't separate. Serve immediately with chicken.

Firecracker Pork

SERVES FOUR

2 whole pork tenderloins, cleaned of silver skin
and marinated (see recipe below) for at least
24 hours to get meat nice and spicy

3 carrots, cut julienne

2 stalks of leeks, cut julienne

6 stalks celery, peeled and cut julienne

4 to 6 button mushrooms, washed and quartered

4 to 6 shiitake mushrooms,
washed and cut julienne

2 cups fresh spinach, trimmed and washed

1 cup chicken stock

1/2 cup pork marinade

2 cups bow-tie pasta, cooked

1 teaspoon diced ginger

1 teaspoon diced garlic

1/2 teaspoon diced shallot

1 tablespoon sesame oil

Salt and pepper to taste

1 cup roasted cashews

Grill pork tenderloin. While pork is cooking, use a 12- to 14-inch sauté pan or wok. Get pan hot. Add sesame oil, garlic, ginger and shallots. Cook for 1 minute. Add carrots, leeks and celery. Add stock and marinade. Simmer 6 to 8 minutes. Add spinach and bow-tie pasta. Place mixture in serving tray. Garnish with sliced roasted pork and roasted cashews.

Firecracker Pork Marinade

MAKES 2 CUPS

1 tablespoons chopped ginger

1 tablespoon chopped garlic

1 teaspoon chopped shallot

1/2 cup tamari

1/2 cup water

1/4 cup sesame oil

2 to 3 red chili peppers (optional)

Place all ingredients in a saucepan. Bring to a boil. Let cool.

Veal Champignon with Truffle Butter

SERVES FOUR

This is a very elegant dish. We use prime veal tenderloin cut into medallions and lightly pounded into thin filets.

Eight 3-ounce veal medallions

2 whole portobello mushrooms, sliced

12 medium-sized shiitake mushrooms, stems removed and sliced

8 large button mushrooms, sliced

12 fresh morel mushrooms (optional)

2 teaspoons shallots

1 teaspoon Italian truffle butter (available in gourmet food stores)

8 ounces whole cream

8 ounces beef or veal stock

4 ounces brandy

2 cups flour

1 cup flour for dredging

Place 6 ounces of truffle butter into a 10- to 12-inch sauté pan. Season veal lightly with salt and pepper. Dust veal with flour. Sauté lightly over medium heat on both sides. Take veal out of pan to rest and put in warm place. Add shallots, mushrooms and brandy to sauté pan, and flame off brandy. Add cream and reduce by half. Add stock and reduce until gravy like. Place veal on warm plate, stir in 1 teaspoon of truffle butter. Season with salt and pepper. Pour sauce over veal and serve with your favorite vegetable.

Windows' Rack of Lamb Gourmet

SERVES FOUR TO SIX

This rack of lamb is one of the most wonderful presentations of lamb and also one of the tastiest. The rack is fully Frenched, marinated in olive oil, salt and pepper. When Mr. Zimmerman orders, he insists on his mint jelly.

2 whole 8-bone Frenched racks of lamb (butchers can prepare this)

2 large portobello mushrooms, washed and de-stemmed

4 ounces virgin olive oil

2 teaspoons chopped shallots

2 tablespoons chopped garlic

20-24 whole peeled garlic cloves

3-4 sprigs fresh rosemary

3 cups of excellent port wine

3 ounces lamb stock or beef bouillon

White pepper and salt to taste

In a 2-quart sauce pot, add 2 ounces of olive oil. Get hot and add chopped garlic and shallots. Sizzle for up to one minute. Add cleaned mushrooms and port wine. Let simmer for 10 to 12 minutes, then add 2 to 3 sprigs of rosemary and the stock. Simmer for 15 minutes.

While sauce is simmering, season racks with olive oil, salt and pepper. Place racks on hot grill, sear and turn frequently to keep lamb from burning or catching on fire (been there, done that). Once the lamb has been seared you can finish roasting in the oven to desired temperature at 350 degrees: 6 to 8 minutes for rare; 10 to 12 minutes for medium; 15 to 20 minutes for well done.

While lamb is roasting, place whole garlic cloves in oven and roast until golden brown. To serve, season sauce, slice mushrooms and place on platter with sauce. Slice rack into chops, garnish with roasted garlic and fresh rosemary sprigs. Enjoy!

Rack of Lamb

Veal Winn Dixie

SERVES FOUR

Eight 3-ounce medallions of veal tenderloin, cleaned and lightly pounded out

1½ cups whole unsalted butter

1 cup all-purpose flour

20 jumbo shrimp, peeled and deveined

2 blanched lobster tails, cut in half-lengthwise and removed from shell

4 artichoke bottoms, cooked and cleaned

2 teaspoons chopped jalapeño

½ teaspoon chopped shallots

8 large button mushrooms, washed and quartered

1 cup white wine

Juice of two lemons

1 teaspoon Creole seasoning

White pepper and salt to taste

In a 12- to 14-inch sauté pan, add ¼ cup butter and get hot. Lightly season veal with Creole seasoning, dredge in flour, shake off excess and gently sauté. When veal is cooked on both sides, remove meat from sauté pan and set aside in a warm place. Pour out excess fat. Add shallots, jalapeño, shrimp, mushrooms and white wine. Simmer until shrimp is cooked. Cut artichokes julienne style and add to mixture. Add blanched lobster. Keep ingredients on a very low simmer. Slowly add remaining pieces of whole butter while gently stirring to incorporate butter into sauce to make it creamy looking. Season with lemon juice, salt and pepper, and serve over veal.

Veal Winn Dixie

Tournedo Nicholas

SERVES FOUR

This entrée is another one of Windows' signature dishes. Over the years we have tried many beef tournedo dishes and many variations of this particular dish, but by popular demand, tournedo Nicholas always wins out. I named this dish after my son Nicholas, who is big, beefy and really mellow. The name suits the entrée.

I use only the center-cut 10- to 12-ounce filets for this dish, cut off the whole beef tenderloin. Prime center-cut beef can be special ordered from butchers.

Four 10- to 12-ounce center-cut choice filet mignon

8 ounces Dry Cure 81 ham, cut in $^1/_2$-inch cubes

3 cups rich mellow burgundy wine

2 teaspoons diced shallots

$^1/_4$ teaspoon vegetable oil

12 ounces button mushrooms, washed and quartered

2 cups beef stock or beef bouillon

2 tablespoons whole butter

White pepper and salt to taste

Preheat oven to 400 degrees.

Use a heavy-duty 10- to 12-inch sauté pan or skillet. Place oil in the pan. It should be smoking hot. Season filets with salt and pepper. Sear filets in pan. Turn filets in pan frequently, until you have a $^1/_{16}$-to $^1/_8$-inch crust around the whole filet. This process is used to sear in the juices of the meat. Once the filets have been seared, take out of sauté pan and finish roasting filets in a 400-degree oven. For medium-rare, roast 8 minutes; for medium, up to 15 minutes; and for well-done, up to 30 minutes. While filets are roasting, deglaze pan with shallots and red wine. Reduce by half. Add beef stock and mushrooms. Simmer for 6 to 8 minutes. To finish sauce, add diced ham and simmer 1 minute. Stir in whole butter and season with salt and pepper. Serve.

Tournedo Nicholas

Tournedo China Doll

SERVES FOUR

Four 10- to 12-ounce center-cut choice beef tenderloin

1 teaspoon vegetable oil

8 ounces fresh foie gras, slice in 4 equal portions

3 ounces black truffle butter

1 teaspoon finely diced shallots

4 ounces fine brandy

White pepper and salt to taste

8 ounces fresh morel mushrooms, cleaned and trimmed

3 ounces unsalted butter

Use a heavy-duty 10- to 12-inch sauté pan. Season beef filets with salt and white pepper. Put the sauté pan on high and get hot. Add oil and sear filets on all sides until they develop a light crust. Place filet in oven and roast at 350 degrees to desired temperature. Set sauté pan aside for later. In a separate sauté pan, add unsalted butter. Melt slowly until it starts to sizzle. Season morels lightly with white pepper and salt. Sauté morels in sizzling butter until they get slightly crispy. It is okay if butter browns slightly because the nutty flavor will complement the morels. Place sautéed mushrooms in the oven to finish cooking until the meat is done. Take original sauté pan and discard old fat. Add truffle butter and sizzle sauté foie gras on each side. Place sautéed foie gras on top of filet. Add diced shallots to saucepan. Add brandy and flame. Season. Pour over top of filet. Garnish the rim of the plate with morels.

Dressings, Vegetables and Salads

Fresh northern Michigan vegetables abound from the middle of May through the first week of October. During that time, morel mushrooms dot the region's forests, asparagus sprouts at the local Per-Clin orchards, and The Tomato Shop in Northport grows its flowery, butter-sweet Bibb lettuce and prized juicy, succulent tomatoes. Mike Werp, a Buckley-area farmer, grows an assortment of garden delights: beautiful baby green beans, little flying saucer-shaped yellow and green squash known as petite pan, baby flowering zucchini and yellow squash, and assortments of oak lettuces, red romaine and escaroles. Picked in the morning and served at the restaurant the same evening, it is absolutely wonderful. Mike spends many hours toiling to harvest some fantastic vegetables while battling the elements: rain, drought and lots of deer who want to eat the fruits of his labor.

When we serve entrées at Windows, we try to present an assortment of fresh steamed, puréed, blanched, baked or sautéed vegetables. Fresh vegetable preparation is very simple and very complimentary to almost any choice of entrée.

Windows' House Dressing

MAKES ABOUT 1 QUART

This dressing recipe is delicious. At Windows, we use this for our romaine house salad. When we cut our romaine we use only the hearts and center-cut pieces, and we always cut out the lettuce ribs. The recipe calls for vegetable oil, champagne vinegar and Parmesan cheese. You may substitute many kinds of oils, vinegars and cheeses.

3 whole eggs

3 cups salad oil

1/4 cup champagne vinegar

1 teaspoon salt

1 teaspoon cracked black pepper

1/8 cup finely diced onion (optional)

Parmesan cheese to taste

Place whole eggs in mixing bowl (without the shells). Place on high speed or whip by hand with a piano wire whip. Slowly add the oil so it creates an emulsification and continue until all of the oil is incorporated. Once the actual "mayonnaise" is finished, mix or stir remaining ingredients into dressing.

To serve, place cut, trimmed and washed Romaine lettuce in bowl, pour some dressing on top, mix well with tongs. Add Parmesan cheese to taste. Some variations of this salad: rub bowl first with fresh chopped garlic, then add lettuce and dressing. The blue-veined cheeses also add an interesting twist to the salad.

Windows' House Salad

SERVES FOUR TO SIX

1 1/2 cups house dressing

3 heads romaine lettuce

*3 tablespoons fresh
grated Parmesan cheese*

Remove any old romaine leaves and trim tops to remove bruised leaves or bitter ends. Cut off bases of romaine. Separate leaves. Cut out ribs and cut leaves in half or thirds. Leave small hearts of romain whole. Soak lettuce in bowl of cold water for 5 minutes. Pull out lettuce and place in salad spinner to remove excess water. When leaves are mostly dry, place in salad bowl, add dressing and Parmesan cheese. Mix with tongs and serve immediately.

Northport Tomatoes
With Bibb Lettuce, Fresh Mozzarella, Toasted Pine Nuts and Pesto Dressing

SERVES FOUR TO SIX

6 medium ripe Northport tomatoes

3 heads Bibb lettuce

Three 2-ounce balls fresh mozzarella cheese

1 cup toasted light brown pine nuts

1/2 cup Italian pesto

1 cup Windows' house dressing
(see recipe on previous page)

1 ounce grated Parmesan cheese

12 to 16 fresh basil leaves

Make dressing first by mixing house dressing, pesto and Parmesan cheese until incorporated. Taste. You may want to adjust the dressing. Add a little more pesto? More cheese?

Place Bibb lettuce leaves on plate. Core tomatoes and cut into wedges. Place 4 to 5 tomato slices on half the plate. Pour dressing in front of the tomatoes. Slice mozzarella cheese and place in front of sauce. Garnish with fresh basil leaves and toasted pine nuts.

Northport Bibb Lettuce Salad
With Dried Cherries, Pecans, Stilton Blue Cheese, Citrus Vinaigrette

SERVES FOUR TO SIX

4 heads Northport Bibb lettuce

2 cups dried cherries

2 cups toasted pecan pieces

Six 1-ounce balls of Stilton blue cheese

Place large leaves of Bibb lettuce on plate. Take hearts and slice julienne and place in center of plate. Liberally sprinkle pecans and cherries on plate. Drizzle dressing and garnish with Stilton cheese ball.

Citrus Vinaigrette Dressing

MAKES 2 CUPS

½ cup Dijon mustard

1½ cup olive oil

1 ounce fresh lemon juice

3 ounces fresh orange juice

White pepper and salt to taste

Place mustard in bowl and slowly beat in olive oil with a wire whip. When incorporated, add lemon and orange juices and season to taste.

Rutabaga Purée

This recipe is used regularly on our plate garnishes. We keep it warm in a pastry bag and squirt some on a plate and use this purée as a base to hold other vegetables in, like cauliflower, sugar snap peas or rosemary sprigs.

½ pound rutabaga

¼ pound carrot

¼ pound potato

(Or desired amount: ½ rutabaga to ¼ carrot and ¼ potato)

White pepper and salt to taste

Whole butter (optional)

Peel, clean and cut all vegetables in 2- to 3-inch rough cut chunks and place them in a pot of water. Bringing to a slow boil, let simmer 30-45 minutes or until vegetables are tender. Once cooked pour into a strainer and drain. If desired, roast vegetables for 15-20 minutes at 330 degrees to steam off some of the water. Puree vegetables and season to taste with salt and white pepper. A little whole butter can be added to make it a little richer.

Green Beans

When I was attending Schoolcraft College in southeastern Michigan, my biker roommate would open a can of green beans, bring them to a boil and continue to let them stew while he took a shower and got dressed. He'd scoop the poor hapless beans onto his plate next to the Banquet fried chicken. We at Windows strive to try to serve a little different green bean.

We take the beans whole and drop them in a boiling pot of water and cook for several minutes until they are al dente, or slightly crispy but cooked. We scoop the beans out into an ice bath to cool. We then trim the beans, snipping off the stems. If the beans are small we just drop them in the steamer or a pot of boiling water and garnish the entree at the last minute for the guest. If the beans are a little more meaty, we sizzle finely diced shallots in whole unsalted butter, add blanched beans and season with salt and white pepper and serve.

Asparagus

We peel asparagus stems due to the stringy nature of the vegetable. Then we tie 12 to 14 asparagus together with butcher twine and blanch the entire bunch with the same cooking technique that we use for green beans.

Squash and Zucchini

Petite pan squash, baby zucchini and yellow squashes should be steamed so that when the entrée is served, it can be garnished at the last second.

Carrots

Carrots have been an item of controversy over the years: should they be cut in ovals, rounds or on the bias? Perfect little eight-sided carrots? Julienne, batard or brunoise? We at Windows have had carrots sent back to the kitchen because they were too hard for some poor carrot-loving soul. "There is nothing wrong with these carrots—they are cooked al dente," we would bellow out to the wait staff.

My favorite recipe for carrots is my mom's.

Mom's Carrots

1 pound carrots (or desired amount)

2 tablespoons unsalted butter

1 teaspoon fresh dill, chopped

2 teaspoons honey

Steam carrots until tender. Cool in an ice bath. Then slightly simmer in unsalted butter, fresh chopped dill and honey.

Fall Vegetables

Our fall vegetable selection is delicious. We make soup with butternut squash. We coat wedges of acorn squash with Michigan maple syrup, roasted and filled with rutabaga purée. We cut spaghetti squash in half and remove the seeds, then place it skin side up and bake it in a roasting pan with a little water. When the squash is tender, after about 45 minutes, we let it cool. We then scrape out the squash meat with a fork, and it looks like spaghetti. Cook it in butter, steam it or roast it with fish or fowl.

During the winter months we are at the mercy of out-of-state growers and have to be selective with vegetables. I once tried some of the newer invented vegetables, such as broccoflower. Broccoflower? Did broccoli and cauliflower have a choice to get together? It tasted like straw. When broccoli met asparagus, they called it "broccolini."

Broccolini

(SUNG TO THE RHYTHM OF "THE BRADY BUNCH")

One day when this broccoli met this asparagus,

They grew together and they fell in love.

There was broccoli and asparagus everywhere.

So they got together and made the broccolini bunch.

The broccolini bunch, the broccolini bunch.

They grew together with genetic engineering,

With nutrition and tastiness for all.

The broccolini bunch.

The broccolini bunch ...

Dauphinoise Potatoes
Windows' House Potatoes

SERVES SIX TO EIGHT

6 large baker potatoes, peeled

2 teaspoons garlic

1½ cups whole cream

½ cup milk

½ teaspoon salt

¼ teaspoon white pepper

1¾ cup grated Gruyere cheese

2¼ cup grated cheddar cheese

Mix whole cream, milk, salt and pepper and set aside. Mix grated Gruyere and cheddar cheese together and set aside. Spread all chopped garlic on the bottom and sides of a 2-quart casserole dish. Slice potatoes ⅛-inch thick right into the casserole dish. If you do not have a mandoline, you can slice potatoes very thin with a French knife.

Once potatoes are sliced, pour cream and milk mixture over top. Place grated cheeses on top. Bake in a 350-degree oven for 45 minute to 1 hour, or until top is golden brown. Test potatoes with a paring knife to ensure they are soft. Let cool 10 minutes before serving.

Grilled Fall Vegetables
With a Roasted Garlic and Maple Syrup Vinaigrette

SERVES FOUR TO SIX

3 medium zucchini, cleaned and
cut lengthwise into ¼-inch strips

4 cups whole peeled garlic cloves

2 onions, peeled and cut into ½-inch round rings

1 dozen shallots, peeled

3 peppers, 1 each of red, yellow,
green, washed and left whole

White pepper and salt to taste

2 tablespoons olive oil

Season all vegetables above with olive oil, salt and pepper

3 heads Bibb lettuce

1½ cups olive oil

½ cup whole-grain mustard

½ cup balsamic vinegar

1 cup Michigan maple syrup

White pepper and salt to taste

Preheat oven to 350 degrees.

On a hot grill, sear off sweet peppers and roast in oven for 8 to 10 minutes until tender and skin starts to come loose. When peppers are cooked, place in a covered container to cool. Roast garlic cloves and shallots at 350 degrees until golden brown and tender. Grill zucchini strips about 1 minute on each side and let cool. Grill onion rings and finish in oven for 8 to 10 minutes.

When peppers cool, cut in half, scrape out seeds, scrape off skin, cut in julienne strips and set aside. When all vegetables are cooked, cool and set aside. Set aside about 24 whole garlic cloves.

Purée or finely chop the remaining roasted garlic. Place whole-grain mustard in a bowl, start to whip with a wire whip and slowly incorporate the olive oil. Stir in chopped garlic. Add vinegar and maple syrup. Season dressing to taste.

Place Bibb lettuce on plates, roll zucchini, and garnish plates with remaining roasted vegetables.

Ratatouille

MAKES ABOUT 12 GALLONS

1 bushel or 24 eggplants

4 lemons

15 pounds zucchini

12 Spanish onions

12 pounds assorted red, yellow and green peppers

6 cups finely diced garlic

3 cups finely diced shallots

1½ cups thyme leaves

1 cup oregano leaves

1 cup rosemary leaves

3 cups olive oil

3 quarts tomato juice

15 pounds plum tomatoes

6 cups fine Italian sweet tomato paste

2 cups white wine

½ cup ground white pepper

½ cup salt

3 or 4 gallon pots with lids

Peel eggplant and dice in ½-to ¾-inch pieces. Soak in water with ½ cup salt and juice of four lemons. Let soak until ready to cook. Dice onions, zucchini and peppers into ½- to ¾-inch pieces. Keep separate. Heat pot with 1 cup olive oil. Add onions and caramelize 10 to 12 minutes. Add sweet peppers, zucchini, plum tomatoes, tomato juice, garlic, shallots, white wine and herbs. Bring to a simmer or low boil on stove, add eggplant. Braise in oven at 350 degrees for 35 to 40 minutes.

Desserts

Chocolate Pâté

SERVES EIGHT

6 ounces coffee

³/₄ cup sugar

10 ounces dark chocolate

6 ounces butter

5 eggs

Melt chocolate and butter in double boiler. Set aside. Boil coffee and sugar together and add to chocolate mixture. Whip eggs, one at a time, into chocolate. Insert in a water bath and bake for 60 minutes or until firm. Bake at 325 degrees in a foil-covered pan. Best served warm with fresh whipped cream.

Chocolate Pâté

Chocolate Cherry Terrine

Serves twelve

9 ounces dark chocolate

4 ounces butter

$1/8$ cup cocoa powder

5 egg yolks

$1/3$ cup sugar

5 egg whites

$1/2$ cup whole cream—lightly whipped—soft peaks

1 cup dried cherries, poached in simple syrup and strained

Place chocolate, butter and cocoa powder in a medium-sized bowl over a pot of warm water. Stir and melt slowly. When completely melted, set aside. Whip egg yolks and sugar with mixer on high speed. Once ribbons form and triple in volume, fold into melted chocolate mixture. Whip egg whites to soft peaks. Fold into chocolate mixture. Fold in lightly whipped cream. Lastly, fold in poached dried cherries. To mold, use a terrine pan lined with plastic wrap. Pour in chocolate mixture. Freeze overnight.

To serve, place warm chocolate sauce or fruit sauce on plate. Slice Terrine and place on top of sauce.

Garnish

$1/2$ cup dried cherries

$1/2$ ounce sifted powder sugar

Garnish with dried cherries and powered sugar.

Warm Chocolate Sauce

MAKES 12 OUNCES

8 ounces chopped dark bittersweet chocolate

4 ounces whole cream

First, scald cream and pour over chocolate. Stir until melted. Take terrine out of pan, slice and set in a pool of warm chocolate sauce.

Chocolate Cherry Terrine

Chocolate Mousse Olivia

SERVES SIX

5 ounces white chocolate

6 ounces dark chocolate

6 ounces butter, cubed

6 eggs, separated

Melt both chocolates separately in double boiler. Add cubed butter to dark chocolate, stirring until blended. Remove from heat and beat in yolks. Return to heat and raise temperature to 120 degrees. Remove from heat and cool to 80 degrees. Whip egg whites until soft peaks form, then slowly fold egg whites into dark chocolate mixture. Chill.

Take melted white chocolate and stripe 2 sheets of 5-by-12 parchment. Cool until manageable. Fold short side over to opposite short side in order to create hollow lattice tube. Chill. Fill with mousse. Peel off parchment. Chill and serve on raspberry coulis.

Raspberry Coulis

2 pints raspberries

2 cups sugar

1 cup water

Bring raspberries, sugar and water to boil and simmer for 6 minutes. Purée and strain. Chill and serve.

Chocolate Mousse Olivia

Chocolate Raspberry Mousse Torte

SERVES TEN TO TWELVE

Chocolate Cake

9 eggs

1¹/₈ cups granulated sugar

¹/₂ cup all-purpose flour

¹/₂ cup cake flour

¹/₂ cup excellent cocoa powder

3¹/₂ ounces unsalted butter

2 pints fresh raspberries

Place eggs and sugar in mixing bowl. Place bowl over double boiler and stir until sugar and egg mixture becomes lukewarm. Place mixture of eggs and sugar on high speed. Whip until almost tripled in volume or until stiff peaks form, about 6 to 8 minutes. Meantime, lightly butter a 10-inch cake pan and dust inside with flour. Preheat oven to 350 degrees. Fold flour into batter, sifting it in. Fold in cocoa powder. After all dry ingredients are folded in, pour in remaining melted butter. Mix until just incorporated. Pour batter into cake pan. Bake 25 to 30 minutes. Cool cake. Set aside 2 pints of raspberries.

Ganache

16 ounces fine European dark bittersweet chocolate

4 1/2 ounces whole unsalted butter

5 cups cream

Chop chocolate and place in bowl with butter. Scald cream. Let rise once. Add to chocolate and butter and slowly stir with spoon until incorporated. Be careful not to produce any air bubbles. Cool to room temperature or until tepid.

Chocolate Mousse

6 ounces fine European dark bittersweet chocolate

1 1/2 cups whole cream

Melt chocolate slowly over double boiler. If steam is coming out, the chocolate is melting too fast. Once melted, let chocolate cool slightly to the warmth of baby milk. Whip whole cream to medium peaks. Temper whipped cream into melted chocolate. Finish folding in chocolate until completely incorporated. Refrigerate and let mousse set.

Assembling the Torte

Take cake out of pan. Slice twice to get three thin circles. Place one third of choco-late mousse in center of first cake circle. With spatula, very carefully spread mousse within an inch of the cake edge. Place $^1/_2$ pint of raspberries on top of mousse. Repeat with second cake circle. Place third cake circle on top. Spread remaining mousse all around cake. Refrigerate. Let set for 30 minutes. The ganache should still be pourable and liquid, without being too runny. Pour ganache over center of cake. Let gravity flow the ganache. Once the ganache has dripped down the sides of the cake, smooth outsides with cake spatula. The top of the cake should be smooth and shiny. Take remaining ganache and let it stiffen. Place in a star-tipped pastry bag and decorate top of cake. Place remaining raspberries on top of cake.

Chocolate Raspberry Mousse Torte

Creme Caramels

MAKES SIX 6-OUNCE CUPS

Caramel Base

7 ounces sugar

2 ounces water

Slowly cook sugar and water until light brown, preferably in a copper pot. Pour caramel about $^1/_2$-inch deep into the six 6-ounce cups.

Custard Mix

MAKES SIX SERVINGS

10 ounces milk

10 ounces cream

1 fresh vanilla bean, split

$^1/_2$ teaspoon orange zest

7 eggs

4 ounces sugar

Juice from 2 oranges

Place split bean, milk, cream and orange zest into pot and scald. Scrape inside out of bean into cream mixture. Preheat oven to 275 degrees. Whip together eggs, sugar and juice from oranges. Slowly add cream mixture to the egg mix. Strain and pour into six caramel-based cups. Place into water bath and bake for 90 minutes or until firm.

Creme Caramel

Pecan Cheesecake

SERVES TEN TO TWELVE

Crust

1 pound Graham cracker crumbs

6 ounces melted unsalted butter

Preheat oven to 300 degrees.

Mix graham cracker crumbs with melted butter, press into 10-inch pie pan. Add cream cheese filling.

Filling

2 pounds cream cheese	*3 eggs*
2 cups brown sugar	*1 cup pecan pieces*
1 tablespoon all-purpose flour	

Mix brown sugar and flour. Cream the cream cheese. Scrape down bowl. Once cheese is creamed and smooth, add brown sugar and flour mixture. While mixing add eggs one at a time. When incorporated, scrape down bowl. To make sure that it is mixed well, add pecan pieces at the end. Place in crust. Bake for 90 minutes or until firm. Cool.

Sour Cream Topping

½ pound cream cheese	*3 ounces sugar*
4 ounces sour cream	*24 pecan halves*

Blend together sour cream and cream cheese, spread evenly over top of cooked and cooled cheesecake. Score cake by 12 and place 2 pecan halves on each slice.

Pecan Cheesecake

Shortbread

This shortbread recipe originated with the Stibble family in Scotland through one of my ancestors, via my mother's first cousin, whom we called Aunt Marge. At Christmastime, Aunt Marge would bring shortbread pie. We would break off chunks and eat it. Al, Marge's husband, ate it with sharp cheddar cheese. Shortbread was one of the treats that everyone coveted during the holidays.

When I called my mother to get Aunt Marge's shortbread recipe, I was told fat chance of acquiring it because it was secret. Aunt Marge would not even give it to my mother. So I called Aunt Marge to ask for the recipe. She was at first a little leery of my request. When I told her that I wanted to use the recipe in the restaurant, Aunt Marge and Al came to Windows for dinner. I did get the recipe. I also got the picture of the Stibble family shop where the recipe was created. I shared the recipe with my mother the moment I received it.

This shortbread has many versatile uses. We form it thinly in a pie pan and bake it until tender and still white. Then, we pour in chocolate lemon ganache, let it set, and slice it like pie. We also roll it into a log and slice $1/2$-inch circles, which are baked into cookies. This recipe also makes great dough for Christmas cookies.

J. Stibbles

Dark Chocolate Lemon Shortbread Tart

SERVES EIGHT TO TEN

Shortbread Tart

4 ounces unsalted butter, room temperature

1 cup all-purpose flour

$1/4$ cup light brown sugar

Cut butter in cubes. Knead together flour, sugar and butter until dough becomes solid. Form into a 10-inch tart shell pan. Use fork to lightly place a few intermittent holes in dough. Bake at 325 degrees for 17 to 20 minutes. The perfectly cooked shortbread tart should be as white as possible. Let tart cool. When cooled, pour in filling, such as chocolate lemon ganache (see recipe on next page).

Chocolate Lemon Ganache

Serves twelve

1 egg yolk	2 tablespoons lemon zest
$^{1}/_{4}$ cup sugar	3 ounces fresh-squeezed lemon juice
$^{1}/_{4}$ cup heavy cream	9 ounces bittersweet chocolate (or substitute white or milk chocolate)

Chop chocolate and place in bowl. Whip yolk and sugar at high speed. Scald cream and lemon zest. Temper whipped yolk and sugar into scalded cream. Slowly stir in lemon juice. Place mixture in a pot, stir vigorously while cooking to just the boiling point. Strain mixture onto chocolate. Stir until fully incorporated. Pour mixture into cooked shortbread tart shell. Let cool until chocolate mixture is set. This dessert keeps well and can be made days ahead of time.

Chocolate Lemon Shortbread Tart

Princess Gabrielle

SERVES SIX

Cream Puffs

MAKES TWELVE PUFFS

9 ounces water

1 teaspoon salt

3½ ounces butter

6½ ounces flour

5 eggs

Preheat oven to 375 degrees.

Bring water, salt and butter to a boil. Stir in sifted flour until single mass forms. Place in mixing bowl. Using electric mixer, beat at low speed for five minutes. While mixing, add 4 eggs, one at a time, beating continuously. Using pastry bag, pipe onto greased or parchment paper-covered baking sheet. Break up last egg and egg wash each puff. Bake for 35 to 45 minutes until golden brown.

Princess Gabrielle Topping

SERVES SIX

6 scoops vanilla ice cream

6 scoops chocolate-raspberry ice cream

6 ounces chocolate sauce

6 ounces raspberry sauce

Warm cream puff shells, split in half, fill with ice cream, garnish with sauces and fresh whipped cream.

Princess Gabrielle

Mucho Mocha
Milk Chocolate Mocha Ice Cream

MAKES A HALF GALLON

8 egg yolks

3/4 cup sugar

1 pint milk

1 pint heavy cream

12 ounces milk chocolate

1/2 cup espresso

Melt chocolate and espresso over double boiler. Set aside.

With mixer at high speed, whip together egg yolks and sugar until pale, ribbony and tripled in volume. Place cream and milk into a thick-bottomed pot, slowly scald and bring to a single scald rise. With mixer on low speed, slowly add scalded cream and milk into the egg and sugar mixture to fully temper. Once fully incorporated, place entire mixture on a simmering pot of water. Add melted chocolate and coffee, stir over pot of water for 8 to 10 minutes. Run through ice cream machine.

Mucho Mocha

White Chocolate Dried Cherry Ice Cream

MAKES A HALF GALLON

8 egg yolks

$^3/_4$ cup sugar

1 pint milk

1 pint cream

14 ounces white chocolate

$1^1/_2$ cups dried cherries

Poach dried cherries in simple syrup and strain. Whip egg yolks and sugar on high-speed mixer until it doubles in volume. Bring milk and cream to a boil; temper into sugar and egg mixture. Melt white chocolate over double boiler and add to mixture. Stir for at least one minute over double boiler. Run through ice cream machine and when ice cream is done, mix in poached cherries. Put it in the freezer to set.

Jack Daniel's Ice Cream

MAKES A HALF GALLON

8 egg yolks

$^3/_4$ cup sugar

1 pint milk

1 pint heavy cream

18 ounces milk chocolate

$1^1/_2$ ounces Jack Daniel's bourbon

Whip egg yolks and sugar on highspeed until doubled in volume. Scald milk and heavy cream; temper into sugar mixture. Melt chocolate and add to sugar mixture. Add Jack Daniel's. Stir on double boiler for at least 1 minute. Run through ice cream machine. Put in freezer to set.

This recipe is good with friends.

Vanilla Ice Cream

MAKES ONE HALF GALLON

8 egg yolks

1 cup sugar

1 quart heavy cream

1 vanilla bean

Whip egg yolks and sugar on high-speed mixer until doubled in volume. Cut vanilla bean in half. Place heavy cream and halved vanilla bean in a thick-bottomed pot. Bring to boil. Scrape bean into cream. Temper into sugar mixture. Stir for 1 minute over double boiler. Run through ice cream machine. Put in freezer to set. The richest ice cream, in moderation, can make you feel like a king.

Chocolate Raspberry Ice Cream

MAKES ONE HALF GALLON

8 egg yolks	*1 pound dark chocolate*
³/₄ cup sugar	*4 ounces strained raspberry jam*
1 pint milk	*1 pint heavy cream*

Whip egg yolks and sugar on high-speed mixer until doubled in volume. Melt chocolate slowly in a double boiler. Set aside. In a thick-bottomed pot, scald milk, cream and raspberry jam, then add to sugar mixture. Beat by hand or with a mixer. Then add chocolate mixture. Stir for one minute in double boiler. Run through ice cream machine and put in freezer to set.

Chocolate Sauce

12 ounces dark bittersweet chocolate

12 ounces heavy cream

Scald cream and add to chocolate.

Caramel Sauce

12 ounces granulated sugar

4 ounces water

2 cups heavy cream

1 teaspoon vanilla extract

1 teaspoon butter

Combine water and sugar in pot and cook until light golden brown. Slowly add cream while stirring. Add vanilla and butter, stir on low flame for 5 minutes.

Raspberry Sauce

2 cups raspberries (fresh or frozen)

1 cup water

1 cup sugar

Place all ingredients in pot, bring to boil. Simmer for 6 minutes. Strain and chill.

Chocolate Truffles

The truffle recipes included here have proven to be the most popular of Windows' chocolate delicacies. To really enjoy the experience of a fine chocolate, it is imperative to use the best available European chocolate, such as Cocoa Barry or Vahlrona, as well as unsalted butter and fresh whole cream.

The techniques in the following truffle mixes are very similar, starting with chopping the chocolate on a clean and sanitary surface. Chocolate should be chopped so that pieces are small and consistent in size. After chopping the chocolate and desired flavorings, it's time to scald the cream. Simply let the cream come to the boiling point and let it rise once. Only once! Then add the scalded cream right into the chopped chocolate and flavorings. Once the truffle mix is ready, it can be cooled until it begins to harden. Then it's time to make truffles.

The browned butter truffle mix gets very hard and can be set up in a square mold, like a cake pan, then taken out and cut into diamonds, triangles or squares. Other truffle mixtures can be scooped out with small ice cream scoops or spoons. They also can be whipped with a mixer until doubled in volume, then placed in a pastry bag to make stars or kisses.

There are numerous ways to finish and serve truffles. They can be dipped in melted chocolate and rolled in cocoa powder, powdered sugar, toasted chopped pecans, crushed walnuts or coconut. Prepared chocolate shells are available and can be filled with truffle mix. But the most exquisite way to finish chocolate truffles is by dipping them in tempered chocolate.

Tempering chocolate is an art in itself. Keep in mind that, while melting chocolate, the cocoa butter is the most volatile of ingredients. The tempering process is for fine European chocolate, not lower grades of chocolate on the market, which may contain large amounts of paraffin or wax used to stabilize poor quality.

While melting, chocolate looks smooth and velvety, providing that it is melted slowly over a double boiler without being contaminated by any steam or water. If it is a rainy or humid day, do not even attempt to temper chocolate. The tempering process begins with the cooling process. Cocoa butter must cool at the right temperature and the fats—the cocoa butter—must harden back into a shiny glossy finish. Otherwise, the chocolate will bloom and become streaky, cloudy and grainy tasting.

Tempering chocolate takes time and patience. With white chocolate, start with, say, one pound chopped in small consistent pieces. Place two-thirds in a bowl over a double boiler. Slowly start to melt. If steam comes out anywhere, it will create too much heat and will compromise the chocolate with water.

Gently stir the chocolate until it reaches 82 degrees. If you do not have a thermometer, test the chocolate on your lower lip or inner wrist. It should be tepid warm, similar to heating formula for a baby. Once the chocolate reaches 82 degrees, add the remaining white chocolate. Continue to stir until the temperature rises past 84 to 86 degrees. To test, dip a spoon or spatula in the chocolate so a thin coat covers the spoon. Put in refrigerator to harden. Check the sheen and quality. If the chocolate has hardened to a glossy, smooth finish, it is ready to be used. If it has wavy or oily lines or looks cloudy, it's back to the drawing board.

Tempering milk chocolate involves the same techniques, but the temperatures are different. Place two-thirds of the milk chocolate in a double boiler, bringing the temperature to 104 to 113 degrees. Stir in the remaining third of chocolate and work to a temperature of 82 to 84 degrees. Test milk chocolate in the same way as white chocolate.

Tempering dark chocolate is the most difficult. Be patient. Dark chocolate requires a higher temperature to achieve the proper tempering qualities. Take two-thirds of the chopped dark chocolate and melt it to a temperature of 118-122 degrees. Work in the remaining third to a working temperature of 88 to 90 degrees.

Once the chocolate is tempered, be ready to dip chocolates. When I dip, I keep the bowl of chocolate over a pot of warm water. It keeps the temperature longer, enabling a greater working temper life. When dipping truffles, let them drain a little back into the chocolate, and try not to make a big mess.

Working with chocolate is very exciting, rewarding and adventuresome. Chocolate is one of the most versatile and exhilarating foods. Truffle flavors are endless, limited only by imagination. From steeping exotic teas into chocolates to adding exotic nuts and fruits, there is no limit to what can be created with chocolate.

Truffles

Browned Butter

MAKES ABOUT EIGHTEEN 1-OUNCE CHOCOLATES

This is my favorite chocolate. The whole, unsalted butter is melted to a golden dark brown color and then strained on top of the chopped chocolate. This is the truffle that carries the "W" on the chocolate at the restaurant. It is cut into a square.

5 ounces whole cream

5 ounces milk chocolate, chopped

5 ounces dark chocolate, chopped

3^1/$_2$ ounces whole unsalted butter

Place chopped chocolate in a bowl. Place butter in a thick-bottomed sauce pot. Start to cook slowly. In a separate pot, scald cream and pour over chocolate. Stir chocolate and scalded cream. Meanwhile, the butter should be turning a dark golden amber color and starting to have a nutty aroma. Strain browned butter through a fine sieve or china caps. Discard the browned milk solids. Stir golden browned butter into chocolate mixture until fully incorporated. Place in container and let cool. This mixture can get hard in the refrigerator and cut into shapes. Or it can be cooled at room temperature until tepid and put in a mixer at high speed to double in volume, then placed in a pastry bag to make stars or kisses.

Chocolate Raspberry Truffles

MAKES ABOUT EIGHTEEN 1-OUNCE CHOCOLATES

This mixture is very versatile. We have used it chopped into bite-sized pieces to put into chocolate raspberry ice cream. We have whipped it into peaks on the mixer and used it for borders on chocolate raspberry wedding cakes. Or we've scooped it out with small ice cream scoops, dipped it in tempered dark chocolate and decorated it with small pieces of gold leaf.

10 ounces dark bittersweet chocolate, chopped

3 ounces whole unsalted butter, cubed

$^1/_2$ cup whole cream

$^1/_2$ cup pure raspberry jam

Place chopped chocolate in a bowl. Place cubed butter on top of chocolate. Place cream and raspberry jam in a thick-bottomed sauce pot. Scald cream and raspberry jam and stir while heating because the sugar in the jam can easily burn. Once scalded, strain over top of chocolate to remove seeds. Stir until fully incorporated. Let cool. Scoop into 1-ounce balls. Dip in tempered dark chocolate and decorate with gold leaf.

Mocha Truffles

MAKES ABOUT EIGHTEEN 1-OUNCE CHOCOLATES

This truffle is very popular with the coffee nuts. When you bite into this chocolate, it is like getting a shot of double-caf half-caf espresso-cappuccino deluxe. It is dipped in tempered dark chocolate and garnished with an espresso bean.

10 ounces dark bittersweet chocolate, chopped

2 ounces whole unsalted butter

$^1/_2$ cup whole cream

$^1/_2$ cup fresh brewed espresso (amount can vary to taste)

Place chopped chocolate in a bowl, and place butter on top of chocolate. Scald cream and pour over chocolate. Add freshly brewed espresso. Gently stir until fully incorporated. Cool and scoop out truffles.

White Chocolate Lime Truffles

MAKES ABOUT SIXTEEN 1-OUNCE TRUFFLES OR FILLING FOR ONE 10-INCH CAKE

This truffle is a soft mix that works well with filling truffle shells or for cake filling.

6³/₄ ounces white chocolate, chopped

1 ounce granulated sugar

1¹/₂ ounces whole cream

2 egg yolks

Zest from 1 lime

2¹/₄ ounces fresh lime juice

Place chopped white chocolate in bowl. Set aside. Place egg yolks and sugar in electric mixing bowl at high speed until doubled in volume. Then lower speed to slow and slowly add lime juice to mix. Place whole cream and zest in sauce pan. Scald. Then slowly add scalded cream mixture into beaten egg yolks and sugar. Once cream is incorporated into sugar-yolk mixture, place in sauce pot. Bring to scalding point while stirring vigorously. Strain through a sieve or china cap onto white chocolate. Stir and use when cooled.

Pecan Truffle Mix

MAKES ABOUT THIRTY 1-OUNCE CHOCOLATES

This truffle mix has been a work in progress over the years as we tried to get a good chocolate flavor to complement pecans. We tried many variations and finally arrived at this recipe, courtesy of Paul Prudhomme. We take bittersweet French chocolate, whole unsalted butter and fresh cream, and mix it with Paul's recipe for pecan pralines. It is wonderful. This recipe can be found in Paul's first cookbook.

16 ounces dark bittersweet chocolate, chopped

4 ounces whole unsalted butter, cubed

6 ounces whole cream

*1 batch of Paul Prudhomme's recipe for pecan pralines,
minus the pecan halves (just use pieces in this recipe)*

Place chopped bittersweet chocolate in a bowl. Add cubed butter. Scald cream and add to chocolate. Stir until fully incorporated. Make praline mix and cook until it reaches 210 to 220 degrees. Pour over chocolate while hot. Stir until fully mixed. Let cool. Scoop out truffles with a small ice cream scoop.

Truffle Dip

8 ounces unsalted roasted chopped pecan pieces

8 ounces dark bittersweet chocolate, melted

Dip pecan balls in melted chocolate and roll in chopped pecans.

Honey Truffles

MAKES ABOUT TWENTY-FOUR 1-OUNCE CHOCOLATES

Honey truffles are one of the most interesting chocolate taste combinations. This is a really soft truffle mix. It is best with a pungent organic honey. The truffles are scooped out with two teaspoons to make 1-ounce football shapes. They are then rolled in a dark red cocoa powder. This recipe also makes one of the most heavenly cake fillings.

8$^1/_2$ ounces of dark bittersweet chocolate, chopped

6 ounces milk chocolate, chopped

4 ounces organic honey

6 ounces cream

1 cup dark red cocoa powder

Place chopped milk and dark chocolate in bowl. Pour honey on top. Scald cream and pour over chocolate-honey mixture. Let cool. Scoop out truffles and roll in cocoa powder.

Mardi Gras

Since March 1987, Windows has thrown a two-day Mardi Gras party. Usually it is planned the weekend before Mardi Gras Tuesday. This annual event has become so popular that is often sold out six months in advance. We completely decorate the restaurant with green, purple and gold using hundreds of helium balloons, beads and doubloons. There's a festive six-piece band, jugglers, flame throwers and face painters. The staff each year has come up with a costume theme, from being prom queens or Groucho Marx to fairies, bikers and genies.

The food is a grandiose buffet with ice carvings, chocolate sculptures and all the incredible food we serve on our menu throughout the year.

Following are ingredients to provide a Mardi Gras party for 300 of your family and friends.

Mardi Gras Feast

Beverages

25 cases assorted beer

76 bottles assorted red wines

180 bottles of your favorite white wines

6 bottles Absolut vodka

4 bottles Kettle One vodka

8 bottles Chevis Regal

3 bottles Glenlivet

4 bottles Bombay gin

3 bottles Tanqueray gin

2 bottles Makers Mark

3 bottles Tio Pepe tequila

3 bottles Jim Beam

3 bottles kahlua

3 bottles Meyer's rum

1 bottle Tia Maria

2 bottles Grand Marnier

2 bottles courvoissier

30 pounds coffee

Fresh Produce

1 pound fresh chives

2 pounds fresh rosemary

8 ounces fresh thyme

12 bunches parsley

15 pounds fresh garlic, peeled

10 pounds shallots, peeled

10 pounds Belgian endive

12 bunches fresh watercress

8 heads radiccio

5 pounds radishes

6 bunches scallions

6 heads of salad Savoy

3 cases romaine lettuce

6 bunches red leaf lettuce

6 bunches green leaf lettuce

12 heads bibb lettuce

10 pounds green grapes

10 pounds red grapes

3 honey dew melons

3 cantaloupes

5 pounds kumquats

33 kiwi

26 pints fresh strawberries

15 pints fresh raspberries

10 pints fresh blackberries

12 ripe pineapples

10 pounds large button mushrooms

5 pounds portobello mushrooms

6 pounds shiitake mushrooms

5 pounds oyster mushrooms

22 pounds gold peppers

55 pounds green bell peppers

11 pounds red peppers, large

24 large artichokes

40 pounds zucchini

24 eggplants

48 limes

72 lemons

5 pounds red onions

50 pounds yellow onions

24 oranges

50 pounds red potatoes

25 pounds russet potatoes

Meat

4 legs of lamb

6 whole prime ribs

9 pounds dry cure ham

20 pounds mild Andouille sausage

45 pounds beef tenderloin

15 pounds house-made pâtés

Seafood

40 pounds whole king crab legs

150 pounds jumbo shrimp

25 pounds boiled crawfish

40 pounds fresh crawfish tail meat

40 pounds fresh blue lump crabmeat

Fifty 1 1/2-pound live lobsters

Six 3-to 4-pound live lobsters

80 large bluepoint oysters

80 oyster bras d'or

36 cherrystone clams

24 pounds green lip mussels

20 pounds fresh cultivated mussels

30 pounds Icelandic lobster tails

7 3/4 pounds smoked whole salmon

7 1/4 pounds whole smoked lake trout

10 pounds smoked whitefish

5 pounds smoked mackerel

5 pounds smoked chubs

5 pounds smoked rainbow filet

24 pounds dry pack fresh jumbo sea scallops

20 pounds catfish filets

17 1/2 pounds John Dory filets

10 pounds redfish filets

20 pounds monkfish filets

20 pounds sturgeon filets

6 whole Atlantic salmon, dressed

32 1/4 pounds Norwegian salmon filets

20 pounds split stone crab

10 pounds crab cocktail claw

15 pounds lobster tail scampi

10 pounds walleye filet, medium

Poultry

100 pounds duck

24 pounds Amish chicken breasts

Groceries

8 pounds French brie

One 10-pound wheel of Maytag blue cheese

5 pounds chevre

5 pounds Leelanau garlic pepper cheese

10 pounds puff pastry dough

1 gallon white horseradish

3 gallons ketchup

25 pounds rice

2 pounds cracked black pepper

25 pounds beet sugar

1 case whole plum tomatoes

44 pounds dark semi-sweet chocolate

12 pounds white chocolate

14 pounds milk chocolate

1 gallon clarified butter

$^1/_2$ gallon vegetable oil

Twenty-four 4-ounce boxes Bremmer's white crackers

*Two 960-count Carr's table wafer's,
bite-size banquet pack*

Six 3-liter Zoe extra virgin olive oil

Four 5-liter champagne vinegar

Two 4.5-ounce Lahvosh small white crisp bread

10-pound can cornichons

Twelve 15-ounce jars peppercorns in brine

Four 10-pound cans tomato paste

5 pounds Creole spice

Dairy

2 cases heavy whipping cream

1 case Half & Half

30 dozen eggs

4 gallons milk

20 pounds clarified butter

72 pounds butter

10 pounds sharp cheddar

30 pounds cream cheese

10 pounds sour cream

1 pound truffle butter

6 pounds smoked cheddar

18 pounds Stilton

9 pounds Stilton with lemon zest

20 ounces Bourdin goat log

$1^3/_4$ pounds Boursin herb cheese

6 pounds Roquetfort

47 pounds grated Parmesan

36 pounds Gruyere

7 pounds Spanish Cabrales

Non-Food Items

375 purple balloons

375 gold balloons

375 green balloons

500 yards curly green ribbon

500 yards curly purple ribbon

500 yards curly gold or yellow ribbon

2,000 pounds helium

1,000 strings of Mardi Gras beads

1,200 Mardi Gras doubloons

2 Mardi Gras flags

6 Mardi Gras banners

Staff

2 bartenders

3 bussers

2 hosts

1 face painter

6 wait staff

3 food servers

7 chefs

2 dishwashers

One 5-piece band

Mix all ingredients well and have a blast.

Appendix

February 2, 2000

'Memorable Dining'

111 St Jospeh

PO Box 512

Suttons Bay

Michigan 49682

616-271-6222

Dear Phil,

Thank you for conducting the cooking class at the Park Place Hotel last Saturday. As you may know your efforts were part of a fundraising dinner and wine auction last August, at Bay Harbor Resort. This fund raiser raised over $80,000 for the American Cancer Society. Thanks for a job well done.

Once again you dazzled the crowd with your ability to make ordinary ingredients...outstanding. The honey truffles were great. I wanted to walk off with a couple of your pans as well!

It has been a rich experience for me to work down the street from you. I continue to admire your humor, your skill, and value your friendship. Thanks.

Sincerely,

Jim Milliman, Chef/Owner

READERS' CHOICE

Phil Murray (right) and staff once again prove they have the right stuff. His restaurant, Windows, took top honors in the heated competition for Best Restaurant. Windows is known for their seafood dishes (like the delicate salmon with capers, above) as well as their to-die-for desserts.

AWARDS

Elegant entrées, romantic hideaways, stunning vistas, sumptuous feasts. Where, we asked, do you go for food that moves you? Well, the readers have spoken.

Whether the fare be humble or hearty, you've searched out the best food Northern Michigan has to offer, and we're here to dish up the results. In our 15th Annual Readers' Choice Awards, hear the voices of experience and opinions of passionate diners as they reward the worthy. Come, meet the winners, and revel in our region's epicurean abundance.

Photography by Brian Confer

GARY PORTER/The Detroit News

The cooking team at Windows in Traverse City: From left, Ron Ernsberger, Steve Hogan and owner Phil Murray.

UPSTATE TREATS

By Sandra Silfven
News Staff Writer

Northern eateries add flavor to fall

Hermann's sports a fancy front in Cadillac.

TRAVERSE CITY — The trek up north for fall color is more delicious by a coefficient of two — Windows, on M-22, seven miles north of Traverse City, and Hermann's European Cafe in downtown Cadillac.

The first is a 2-year-old eatery right on the bay, serving highly stylized American cooking — and I'm talking upscale. And the second is an Austrian-influenced restaurant where the schnitzel is textbook. Both are in places where you might not expect to use the word cuisine but find it most applicable.

Windows occupies the former Pier 22 where hardly a pane of glass is visible until you enter, and then every wall offers a breathtaking view of gulls playing tag over white-crested waves of the west arm of Grand Traverse Bay. Casual plastic, tablecloths and wood paneling may convey a casual menu, but the food of chef-owner Phil Murray is dead serious.

Murray, 31, who grew up in St. Clair Shores and graduated from Schoolcraft College, earned his toque at Commander's Palace and Louis XIV in New Orleans and a French-Basque restaurant called La Bergerie in Alexandria, Va.

FROM THESE experiences he brings to Windows a charming American style with savory Cajun and French accents. The menu includes corn muffins spiced with jalapeno peppers, and turtle soup done the classic way with veal stock, turtle meat and a ton of Louisiana spices. Plus duck confit with salsify or a tournedos marchand du vin (a beef filet with red wine sauce). The menu is the sort that eggs you on.

Appetizers tease with fluffy lump crab puffs bound with homemade mayonnaise in a seafood-creole sauce. And the turtle soup delivers a spicy thrill equivalent to eating it at the best table at Commander's. In another starter, Oysters Olivia, each succulent sea-dwelling morsel is poised in a pool of tomato-rosemary cream surrounding a slice of grilled eggplant. The thick slab of smoked, creamy whitefish terrine with fresh horseradish sauce is almost too rich ... but, sometimes, you just have to suffer.

Entrees are tickled with Murray's Cajun experiences, too, including the Veal Wynn Dixie that has shrimp, lobster meat and fresh, quartered artichoke hearts perched on escalops of veal in a jalapeno butter sauce. And there's more to the plate — a piping of pureed sweet potatoes plus pea pods, cauliflower, cooked red cabbage, a redskin, a wild mushroom and spears of fresh green and yellow squash.

Palate cleansers aren't sorbets at Windows, but either a dish of fresh fruit or a pseudo-caesar salad minus anchovies and the usual rush of garlic.

IT'S THE desserts, though, where the true heart of the restaurant beats. Murray is a pro with chocolate, as in chocolate pate, chocolate-raspberry ice cream, white chocolate terrine in dark chocolate sauce, chocolate-cherry mousse tort, chocolate truffles, chocolate-dipped strawberries and best of all, a lemon-ganache which is pure chocolate fudge with a lemony edge.

Another plus is the wine list. One side of the card lists the imports and those from California, the other side the local wines. Yes, a whole list of local Michigan wines! All are from the Leelanau Peninsula.

Windows, 7677 W. Bay Shore Dr. (M-22), Traverse City. (616) 941-0100. Dinner only. Tues.-Thurs. 5 to 9 p.m., Fri.-Sat. 5 to 10 p.m., Sun. 5 to 9 p.m. Closed Mon. MC, V. Prices: Appetizers from $2.25 to $6.35; entrees, $8.95 to $17.95.

★★★

What's this? Authentic Austrian tortes and wiener schnitzel in the heart of downtown Cadillac? In a store-

Please see **Treats/3D**

Treats

Upstate eateries add flavor to fall

From page 1D

front where the fare used to be Ursala's Smorgasbord with all you can eat for $3.95?

Viennese-trained Hermann Suhs, who has cooked in London, Bangkok and Kathmandu, decided that mid-life was the time to lead a less hectic existence. So three years ago he settled in his wife's hometown of Cadillac and opened Hermann's European Cafe where he dishes up the best of his overseas experiences without frightening the locals away.

THE RESTAURANT has two pleasant dining rooms outfitted in lace curtains, colorful wall-mounted quilts and polished oak. There's also a deli where Suhs' noted Sacher tortes, strudels, Milwaukee-made sausages and about 200 wines are available for takeout.

Though the menu is a mixture of French, Italian and American flavors, with even a hamburger for the asking, the highlight is the Austrian fare, specifically the veal dishes. More specifically, wiener schnitzel. And I can't remember having it this delicious since my Vienna cafe days in the early '70s.

At Hermann's, the schnitzel is authentic. First of all, it's thin. So thin, it covers an entire dinner plate. It's made from good, tender meat. And — bless it — only dipped in egg and crumbs and fried to a golden brown. It is served with a little lemon on the side. The best schnitzel is the simplest.

Suhs says he buys his veal by the leg and breaks it down himself for the two choicest muscles to slice into cutlets. He pounds them with a flat mallet, not a tenderizing device. Plus, his crumbs are from unseasoned, homemade french bread and lightly toasted before they're applied to the veal. Not so simple, after all.

HE ALSO offers the veal in an "Orloff" version, flamed with brandy and topped with crabmeat, plus "Jaeger" style with wild mushrooms and a light sour cream sauce.

With the veal, one's best choice is Lyonnaise potatoes which are cut in chunks and cooked with caramelized onions for old-country flavor.

But not all is Austrian. At dinner, the poached fish dishes are first rate, often incorporated with a light curry sauce which points up Suhs' Asian experiences. So does his seafood curry with coconut — a sweet, hot curry with large shrimps, crab and scallops over rice.

To cap off the evening, Hermann's offers Austrian blue-blood desserts such as thin, crisp apple strudel and Cardinal Meringue Schnitten. The latter is a slice of baked meringue (even in humid weather, it isn't limp) with lightly sweetened whipped cream. To best savor it, Suhs suggests a cup of coffee called *melange* — like a cappuccino, only creamier.

His most celebrated dessert — the famous chocolate Sacher Torte — is not on the menu. You have to request it. The reason? The price. Suhs apologizes that he has to charge $4.50 for it, but, after all, he explains, it's practically all chocolate. "I have to be careful not to be snobbish and scare people off."

Hermann's European Cafe, 214 N. Mitchell (M-55), Cadillac. (616) 775-9563. Lunch and dinner. Open Mon.-Sat. 11 a.m. to 10 p.m.; starting Oct. 15, Mon.-Thurs. 11 a.m. to 9 p.m., Fri.-Sat. 11 a.m. to 10 p.m. Closed Sun. MC, V. Dinner appetizers from $1.50 to $4.90; sandwiches, $3.95 to $6.50; entrees, $7.95 to $14.

ALVIN OWSLEY
ONE SHELL PLAZA
910 LOUISIANA
HOUSTON, TEXAS 77002-4995

October 28, 1999

Windows
7677 West Bay Shore Drive
Traverse City, Michigan 49684

Gentlemen:

Here is a $2,000 check the proceeds of which are to serve as a deposit.

As you know, any whiff of cilantro will trigger a refund in full.

Very truly yours,

Alvin Owsley

AO:jn
Enclosure

This letter is in reference to Mr. Owsley's 50th wedding anniversary party. I have done a few parties for Mr. Owsley in the past with stern verbal communications with the total disdain for cilantro. This is just the tip of the iceberg, when dealing with catering for large weddings, anniversaries, etc.

Richman on Restaurants

LAFITTE

1310 New Hampshire Ave. NW, in the Hampshire Hotel.
296-7600.

Open for lunch Monday through Friday 11:30 to 2:30, dinner 5:30 to 10:30. Reservations for both recommended. AE, DC, MC, V.
Prices: At lunch appetizers $2.50 to $5.50, main dishes $6.75 to $11.75, table d'hote menu $9.50; at dinner appetizers $3.25 to $5.75, main dishes $8.50 to $16.50, desserts about $4 to $5. Full dinner with wine, tax and tip about $30 to $40 per person.

For several years we have been hearing about the revival of regional cooking in America, but until now the evidence in Washington has been absent. Have patience: The South is rising again. Restaurants specializing in southern food, particularly New Orleans cooking, have opened, are opening, may open.

The first of what we hope is a trend, Lafitte has been serving Cajun and Creole food on New Hampshire Avenue for a few months now and has announced it will add Sunday brunch starting today. At lunchtime in midsummer its tables have been full, quite a feat in Washington, which shows how hungry this city has been for authentic New Orleans cooking, heretofore available, to only a limited extent, at 219 and New Orleans Café.

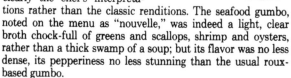

And it does taste authentic, although several dishes are clearly the chef's interpretations rather than the classic renditions. The seafood gumbo, noted on the menu as "nouvelle," was indeed a light, clear broth chock-full of greens and scallops, shrimp and oysters, rather than a thick swamp of a soup; but its flavor was no less dense, its pepperiness no less stunning than the usual roux-based gumbo.

Lafitte's menu, typed daily, changes with the availability of resources. In general, you will find turtle soup and pâté, shrimp or crayfish remoulade, snails and eggplant among the appetizers. At lunch the main dishes include trout—with pecans and creole meunière sauce or with almonds—barbecued shrimp, oysters en brochette and chicken Pontalba. There are usually various preparations of duck and veal. Daily specials might include the Louisiana version of a mixed grill of sausages (andouille, boudin and chorizo) and tasso, a cured, dry meat coated with what tastes like straight cayenne. There is a daily fixed-price lunch that costs $9.50 and includes appetizer, main dish and coffee. Dinner main dishes range from the familiar—rack of lamb or tournedos marchand de vin—to such creole specialties as braised duck with sautéed potatoes and creole mustard sauce, pork confit, shrimp or crayfish étoufée, trout marguery and salmon en croute stuffed with crab, shrimp and scallops.

For Washington, Lafitte is a change of taste. This is gutsy cooking, with seasonings that draw your attention and stay in your memory. The Duck Dumaine had a deep and mellow flavor in its mustard brown sauce, which was absorbed by the sautéed potatoes and mushrooms as well as the meaty, juicy duck. The succulence of the dish was outstanding. The barbecued shrimp was blazing with cayenne, and its clove-and-herb-drenched butter sauce was absorbed by the rice as well as by the fat, juicy and very fresh shrimp. The shrimp in remoulade as appetizer didn't have that same plump quality, but the remoulade sauce is so spunky you ought to at least try it on crayfish if they are available. And the crayfish bisque may

look a benign pink and lull you with its fragrant creaminess, but it sears your tongue as it goes down.

So be warned. If you like your tastes gentle, ask questions before you order. There are mild dishes, too, that were beautifully prepared. The Cajun popcorn-batter-fried crayfish tails were lovely little morsels, although the accompanying sauce was silly, just dijon mustard so far as I could tell, and best ignored. The same mustard also accompanied a tidbit that appeared as we sat down to dinner—breaded fried okra, a delightful surprise—and came on far too strong to be a dip or sauce. Other delicate dishes included baby coho salmon en croute, which achieved that rare balance of flaky, well-cooked crust with moist and properly done fish (its lobster sauce, however, was forgettable). And crayfish or shrimp étoufée were heavy on the garlic but not on the pepper; they tasted rather Italian, their sauce a bright and fresh tomato purée that was a bit on the sweet side but pleasant. The shrimp and crayfish have been impeccable, far superior to those one generally finds in Washington restaurants.

Also rare in Washington is such an interesting choice of à la carte vegetables: There were puréed turnips and fried eggplant in addition to the usual creamed spinach. And there were pommes soufflés, the little puffed potato slices so thin that they are all crust when they expand in the hot oil. They could have been browner but could not have been more perfectly sliced. The salads sound interesting, one of mixed greens in homemade mayonnaise with creole spices, another of surprisingly ripe and flavorful tomatoes with red wine vinaigrette, but in both cases watery greens diluted the dressings to pallidness.

In New Orleans the term lagniappe means a special little bonus. And at Lafitte it means hot muffins—jalapeño cornbread muffins if you are lucky—served as you sit down at lunch, or perhaps the crusty fried okra at dinner. It means a loaf of light french bread wrapped in a napkin and brought to the table as your main dish arrives; it means a pianist playing at lunch as well as at dinner. Main dishes are garnished with some delicious fillips, the best of them being sautéed potatoes and mushrooms with the mixed grill and the duck. The wine list leans heavily toward California, avoids clichés and is priced with restraint.

And now the warnings. Service at Lafitte can be slow. Very slow. It is so hospitable and thoughtful that you might not care a whole lot, for these are waiters and waitresses obviously schooled in southern graciousness. Also, some of the dishes sound more exciting than they taste, particularly the trout with pecans and creole meunière one day, and the sweet potato pecan pie, although that may have been because it was held too long and turned soggy; it might be fine when served fresh. The coffee has been weak, not what one would expect from the New Orleans spirit (although the iced coffee was better than most).

For dessert Lafitte has soufflés but not particularly deft ones; ours was pasty and bland. Investigate the pastry cart, where there is pecan cheesecake and a fruit tart, or the kitchen's own ice creams and sherbets. But above all reserve a piece of the chocolate raspberry torte, which is dense, buttery, fudgy and intensely rich, saved from being cloying by the tart, fresh berries. It is a spectacular bit of chocolate cookery.

All this and a lovely dining room, too, with Art Deco details, flourishes in wood, and mirrors on walls and ceiling. The tables hold not only pretty sprays of exotic flowers but also that most New Orleans of decorations, a bottle of Tabasco on each table.

With Lafitte leading the pack of explorers, Washington is about to discover America.

—**Phyllis C. Richman**

Malcolm and Phil at the St. Charles Hotel in New Orleans, 1980.

Index

Entrées

Dressings, Vegetables and Salads

Order Page

If you would like to order a copy of
Windows Restaurant Cookbook or
order a box of chocolates, please contact:

Windows Restaurant

7677 West Bay Shore Dr.

Traverse City, MI 49684

231-941-0100

or

pmurray@infinitecom.com

visit

www.windowstc.com

❦

WINDOWS RESTAURANT

Book Design by Barbara Hodge

Text Stock is 80 lb. Luna Gloss

Printed by Friesens Book Division

Casebinding by Friesens

Matte finish with spot gloss

Production Editor: Alexander W. Moore, Jr.